Barcelona

D0958032

- A ☞ in the text denotes a highly recommended sight
- A complete A–Z of practical information starts on p.106
- Extensive mapping on cover flaps and throughout text

Berlitz Publishing Company, Inc.

Princeton   Mexico City   Dublin   Eschborn   Singapore

Text:	Donald Allan
Editors:	Christina Jackson
Photography:	Claude Huber
Layout:	Media Content Marketing, Inc.
Cartography:	Cover maps 🌐 Falk-Verlag, Munich; maps on pp. 66 & 75 ©1998 MapQuest.com, Inc.

Thanks to Alfred Bosch, Carlos Sentis, and the staff of the Patronato
Municipal de Turismo in Barcelona for their help in the preparation
of this guide. We would like to thank C. von Brentano, Lydia Aza-
gury, Victoria Béguelin, Parul Subramanian and Dominika von
Zahn for invaluable assistance.

*Although the publisher tries to insure the accuracy of all the
information in this book, changes are inevitable and errors may
result. The publisher cannot be responsible for any resulting loss,
inconvenience, or injury. If you find an error in this guide, please
let the editors know by writing to Berlitz Publishing Company,
400 Alexander Park, Princeton, NJ 08540-6306.*

ISBN 2-8315-6289-9
Revised 1998 – Third Printing April 1999

Printed in Switzerland by Weber SA, Bienne
039/904 RP

CONTENTS

BARCELONA

THE CITY
AND THE PEOPLE

Barcelona is a sophisticated city where the creative energy of modern Europe and the seductive pleasures of the Mediterranean meet in happy union. No one would ever call Barcelona provincial. It may be the second city of Spain, but it ruled an empire before Spain was born.

Protected by the encircling Collserola hills, the city of Barcelona spills down a gentle slope to the sea. Everything from business deals to courting seems to happen on the street in full view, or in the bars open to the street in every block. The avenues are broad and leafy, with open plazas, fountains, and statuary at all the main intersections. Few skyscrapers destroy the human scale of the city profile.

Your first walk down the famous Las Ramblas, half promenade and half bazaar, plunges you into the centre of things. Throngs of Barcelonans are sightseeing here, too, so visitors fit right in. The Ramblas axis will be your point of orientation by day and by night. Ahead is the seaport, to the left is the cathedral and warren of medieval streets, behind is the rectangular grid of 19th-century city planning and the exuberant architecture of Barcelona's unique *Modernisme,* as the Catalans call the city's nationalist interpretation of Art Nouveau.

Far to the right rises Montjuïc, hub of the 1992 Olympics, of great art museums, parks, playgrounds, and the florid buildings of a world fair. This monument to Catalan optimism opened in 1929, just before the stock-market crash.

The fairs of 1888 and 1929 marked bursts of the renewal which periodically thrust Barcelona into new orbits of growth and change, just as the remnants of three rings of concentric walls mark early stages of expansion from the ancient Roman

The bar in Barcelona is office, club, café, and front-row seat.

citadel. The 1992 Olympic Games had the same effect. Selection of the city as the site of the 25th Olympiad set off a multi-billion-dollar building boom that did more than just fulfil the immediate requirements of the games.

New highways were constructed to speed traffic around the centre, the airport and railway stations were upgraded, transport and entertainment facilities, new parks, museums, concert halls, hotels, and office buildings appeared, and new housing revived many rundown neighbourhoods. The activities generated a spirit of pride and optimism, and renovation projects are continuing to rejuvenate both the centre of the city and the outlying districts.

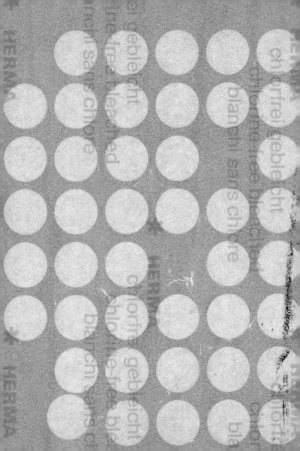

The effect of all this upheaval has been to add yet another layer to several very different Barcelonas of the past. The stones of the Roman city can be seen in columns and walls, and in the archaeological sites you can visit beneath the old Royal Palace. Above this layer is the Barri Gòtic, the walled medieval quarter, very much alive and lived in continuously for over a thousand years. The Eixample, or Expansion, district, laid out when the walls came down in the 19th century, includes the landmark buildings of Modernisme, as well as fashionable boutiques, galleries, restaurants, hotels, and residential blocks.

The Diagonal boulevard cuts the city in half, dividing the older, lower districts from what once were villages at the foot of the hills. These have been absorbed by Barcelona but retain their names—Horta, Gràcia, Sarrià, Pedralbes—and some of their individuality. The fast-growing university district boasts modern buildings, and beyond it on the outer ring are the factories that have made the city prosperous.

Street signs and menus will tell you right away that Barcelona is different from the rest of Spain. Those words with all the x's are Catalan, the language that embodies the separateness and national pride of the seven million Catalan-speaking people, from Perpignan in France to Valencia and the Balearic Islands. Barcelona is the capital of the Autonomous Region of Catalonia, and though both Catalan and Spanish are official languages and most Catalans speak both, the regional government is vigorously promoting Catalan. Over the centuries, outside forces have repeatedly tried—and failed—to suppress Catalan individuality. The most ruthless suppression came during the Franco dictatorship after the 1936–1939 Spanish Civil War, during which Barcelona was a Republican stronghold. Following Franco's death in 1975 Catalonia regained a measure of autonomy, and is enthusiastically rediscovering its culture.

Just over half of the six million Catalans live in Barcelona's metropolitan area. The city proper counts 1.7 million inhabitants, about half of them immigrants or the children of immigrants from the south and other parts of Spain who have come in search of jobs. Many of the people a visitor is most likely to deal with—taxi drivers, hotel and restaurant employees—do not speak Catalan as their mother tongue. Any Spanish remembered from your school days will be useful. But a few courtesy phrases in Catalan will certainly earn you a smile of appreciation.

Barcelona is not only proud of its language, it also boasts a thousand-year-old parliament, an industrial base that produces close to one-fifth of Spain's output, rich monuments of art from antiquity to Gaudí, Miró, and Picasso, swinging entertainment, and a mild climate that attracts millions of sun-seekers from the north the year round. The Olympics capped Barcelona's reputation as a sports-minded community that supports championship golf courses, a top football club, sailing from the harbour, and skiing only a few hours away in the Pyrenees. The golden beaches and turquoise waters of the Costa Dorada and Costa Brava are within easy reach.

Eating, however, is the true local pastime. Barcelonans seem to be eating at all hours of the day and night. And you too will find it hard to resist the temptation of mounds of seafood, clouds of creamy pastries, and ranks of little snack-filled dishes called tapas lined up on the counters of bars. Around 11:00 A.M., a seat at a café table with a *cafe con leche* and a few plates of tapas is the break you'll need to keep going until the customary 2:00 P.M. lunch hour. Follow with a quick siesta until shops and museums reopen at 4:00 or 4:30 P.M.,

The Palau de la Música Catalana's brilliant façade is overwhelmed by exuberant ornamentation.

and by 6:00 or 7:00 P.M. you'll be ready to join the crowds lining the snack bars for another nibble to keep your strength up until 9:30 P.M., the earliest that many restaurants serve dinner. Barcelonans burn up a lot of calories in animated conversation at table, and they expect at least a three-course meal.

Another city emerges at night. The churches, palaces, and monuments are illuminated, fountains dance in veils of colour, and the city's heart beats to a different rhythm. Discotheques, cabarets, and the Ramblas are crowded until very late.

Barcelonans are deeply democratic. The national dance, the *sardana*, epitomises their attitude to life. Men, women, and children holding hands form a circle to perform the intricate steps. There are no solos, but a strong sense of solidarity. People spontaneously dance the *sardana* at all important occasions as if to say, "We are Catalans. You can join our circle, but you cannot break it."

Barcelona at a Glance

Population: Municipality 1.7 million, metropolitan area 3.5 million. Barcelona is Spain's second-largest city after Madrid, and the capital of the Autonomous Region of Catalonia.

Government: The parliament of Catalonia sits in Barcelona; the executive branch of the regional government, the Generalitat, whose head is the President, also has its seat in Barcelona. The province of Barcelona is one of the four that make up Catalonia. The municipal government is run from the Ajuntament, the City Hall.

Economy: With 16 percent of Spain's population, Catalonia produces about 20 percent of the country's Gross National Product, 25 percent of exports, and receives nearly 25 percent of foreign investment. The biggest employer is the automobile manufacturer, SEAT (owned by Volkswagen). After metallurgy, textiles are the main industrial products. From 1992 to 1995 the largest sector of economic growth was "services," of which tourism played a major role.

A BRIEF HISTORY

Tradition holds that Barcelona was first named Barcino, after the Carthaginian general and father of Hannibal, Hamilcar Barca, who established a base here in 237 B.C. Phoenicians and Greeks had settled the coast before then, and Barcino occupied the site of an earlier Celtiberian settlement called Laie. The Romans defeated the Carthaginians in 206 B.C. and ruled Spain for the next 600 years. Roman law, language, and culture took firm root. The Roman citadel in Barcelona, surrounded by a massive wall, occupied high ground where the cathedral and city hall now stand. From the first century A.D. Christian communities began to spread through Catalonia.

After sacking Rome in A.D. 410, the Germanic Visigoths swept into Spain. Barcelona became their capital from 531 to 554, when they moved to Toledo. The invasion of the Moors from Africa in 711 brought the Visigothic kingdom to an end, and Catalonia was briefly overrun. But after their defeat beyond the Pyrenees by the Franks in 732 the Moors withdrew, without ever retaining a lasting foothold in Catalonia. Charlemagne's knights installed themselves in the border counties to guard the southern flank of his empire.

One of these feudal lords, Guifré el Pilós, or Wilfred the Hairy, dominated the rest as Count of Barcelona. He founded a dynasty in 878 that ruled for nearly 500 years. Thus, while much of Spain was under Moorish influence, Barcelona and most of Catalonia remained linked to Europe, a twist of fate that determined the distinct Catalonian character.

The hairy founding father also gave Catalonia its flag of four horizontal red stripes on a gold field, the oldest still in use in Europe. According to legend, the stripes were made in Wilfred's blood, drawn on his shield as an escutcheon by the

The Monument a Colom, in honour of Christopher Columbus, stands above the Plaça del Portal de la Pau.

fingers of the Frankish king after the count had courageously defended his overlord in a battle.

The counts of Barcelona declared their independence when the Frankish king Louis V refused to help repulse Moorish raiders in 988, a date celebrated as Catalonia's birth as a nation-state. The state was soon enlarged through marriages and military adventures. Ramón Berenguer III, the Great (1096 –1131), took Mallorca, Ibiza, and Tarragona from the Moors and acquired the French county of Provence through his wife. His successor, Ramón Berenguer IV, united Catalonia with neighbouring Aragón by marriage, allowing his son Alfonso II to become the first joint Aragón-Catalan king, ruling the Mediterranean coast all the way to Nice. But much of this was lost by the next king, who picked the losing side — a frequent occurrence in Catalan history — in the French crusade against the heretics of Albi.

Succeeding generations then turned towards conquest of the Mediterranean basin. Jaume I, the Conqueror (1213–1276), consolidated control over the Balearic Islands and took Valencia. Pedro III, also the Great (1276–1285), annexed Sicily in 1282. In the next 100 years Barcelona reached the peak of its glory. Its territories included Sardinia, Corsica, Naples, the Roussillon in southern France, and briefly Athens.

These were the centuries of great building in Barcelona, which saw the construction of the cathedral and other great Gothic palaces and monuments. Standing between Europe and the Muslim territories, Barcelona served as a channel for the exchange of scientific knowledge and scholarship. The arts flourished in the cities and monasteries of Catalonia, patronized by a vigorous class of artisans, bankers, and merchants, including an important Jewish community. The beginnings of democratic institutions appeared with a code of laws, the Usatges de Barcelona, in the 11th century, a municipal council with participation of leading citizens called the Consell de Cent, or Council of One Hundred, and in 1283 a parliament, or Corts, for Catalonia, later to become the Generalitat, the civil government.

Barcelona's fate took another decisive turn when the marriage of Ferdinand of Aragón-Catalonia (Ferrán II to the Catalans) to Isabella of Castile joined their two crowns and formed the nucleus of a united Spanish state. Barcelona now was just one of the seats of Los Reyes Católicos, called "The Catholic Monarchs" because in 1492 they finally captured the last Moorish redoubt on the Peninsula at Granada. That same year Christopher Columbus discovered America, thanks to financing from the queen. On his return he was received by the monarchs in the Royal Palace in Barcelona.

That was the last Barcelona saw of the New World's riches for 300 years. Exploitation of the discoveries was the monopoly of the queen's country, Castile, which ever since has been the power centre of Spain. In 1494 the administration of Catalonia was placed under the control of Castile, and the harsh church Inquisition and the expulsion of the Jews were imposed.

The 16th century, a Golden Age for Spain as a whole, saw the political influence of Catalonia and Barcelona decline further. The Dutch-speaking Hapsburg grandson of Ferdinand and Isabella became Charles I of Spain in 1516. A few years later he inherited the title of Holy Roman Emperor as Charles V, with duties throughout Europe that gave him little time for Spain. His son Philip II made previously insignificant Madrid the capital of the great Spanish empire.

As early as 1640 Catalonia declared itself a republic allied to France, with which Spain under Philip IV was then at war. Forced to surrender in 1652, Barcelona saw the Catalan territories north of the Pyrenees delivered to France, fixing the border where it is today. From this point on, Spanish history is a turmoil of constant wars, shifting alliances, and disputes over succession to the crown. In these struggles Barcelona automatically sided with whomever was against Madrid, usually ending up the loser.

The worst of these episodes came in the War of the Spanish Succession (1701–1713) between the backers of Philip of Anjou, the 17-year-old grandson of Louis XIV of France, and the Hapsburg claimant, Archduke Charles of Austria. Charles was enthusiastically received when he landed in Catalonia, but Philip, supported by France, won

The palace where Ferdinand and Isabella met with Columbus upon his return from America.

the war and became the first Bourbon ruler as Philip V. After a 13-month siege, on September 11, 1714, Barcelona was captured and sacked by the royal army. The Catalan Generalitat was dissolved and the city's privileges were abolished. The Ciutadella fortress was built to keep the populace subdued, and official use of the Catalan language

Slicing across the city, the Diagonal boulevard is a showcase of modern architecture.

was outlawed. Typically, Catalonia celebrates this defeat as its national holiday, a symbol of the spirit of resistance.

Trouble for the national government was always an opportunity for the Catalans to rise up — and usually to get slapped down again. From 1808 to 1814 Spain again became a battleground between the English and Napoleon's troops. Catalonia's shrine, the monastery at Montserrat, was destroyed by the French. The sequestration of church properties in Spain in 1835 changed the face of Barcelona, as convents were destroyed and replaced by secular buildings and markets.

The spirit of liberalism abroad in Europe reached Spain tardily. After many reverses, a fairly democratic constitution was proclaimed and constitutional monarchy was installed in 1874. Four years later, Barcelona was at long last given the right to trade with the colonies of the New World.

Meanwhile, the city's energies had been directed to industrialization. Medieval walls were torn down to make way for an elegant modern district, the Eixample, laid out on a grid of broad avenues where the new industrialists built mansions in the latest fashion — Modernisme. Prosperity was accompanied by a revival in Catalan art and literary traditions: La Renaixença. In a burst of optimism, the city bid for worldwide recognition at its Universal Exposition of 1888, built on the site of the hated Ciutadella fortress.

With industrial expansion an urban working class evolved. Agitation for social justice was added to regionalist ferment. Barcelona became the scene of strikes and anarchist violence. The modern Socialist Party and the U.G.T., Spain's largest trade union, were both founded in Barcelona at this time. For their part, the industrialists supported Catalan autonomy as a way to be freed from interference by Madrid. In 1914 a union of the four Catalan provinces, Barcelona, Tarragona, Lleida (Lérida), and Girona (Gerona), was formed, known as the Mancomunitat, with limited autonomy. The region profited from Spanish neutrality in World War I by selling to both sides, further expanding its industry.

The Mancomunitat was dissolved in 1924 by General Primo de Rivera, who set up a military dictatorship and banned the Catalan language yet again. Despite this setback, an optimistic Barcelona plunged energetically into the preparation of an International Exhibition, with monumental buildings, pavilions, and sports facilities erected on the flank of the Montjuïc hill. It opened a few months before the stock market crash of 1929.

In 1931, general elections brought the Republican party to power. King Alfonso XIII went into exile. The next year Catalonia won a charter establishing home rule, restoration of the regional parliament and flag, and recognition of Catalan as the official language of the region. For the next several years the pendulum of power in Spain swung back and forth between Left and Right. The army rebelled in 1936, initiating the bloody Spanish Civil War. Many of

Barcelona's churches were put to the torch by anti-clerical mobs. The city was firmly Republican. In late 1937 it became the capital for a time and a rallying point for the International Brigade. It was one of the last cities to fall to

Catalan

Catalan is a true language, not a dialect of Castilian Spanish. It developed from spoken Latin during the long Roman rule. Catalan has a rich literature from the ninth century to the present. Its closest relative is Provençal, the defunct tongue of southern France. People who understand French and Spanish can make out a good deal of written and spoken Catalan. But two housewives arguing in a market would be comprehensible only to a native.

Outside Catalonia proper, Catalan is spoken in Valencia, Alicante, the Balearic Islands, and north of the French border to Perpignan — some seven million people in all. It is the official language of Andorra.

In the 18th century, King Philip V tried and failed to abolish Catalan to punish the region for supporting a rival to his throne. General Franco's ruthless suppression of the language after the Civil War in 1939 only drove it underground and made it a rallying point of opposition. Under the Constitution of 1978 Catalan is recognized as the mother tongue of Catalonia and as the official language of the Autonomous Region, together with Castilian, the official language of Spain.

Mastery of both Catalan and Castilian is required for graduation from primary and secondary schools. Most public education is in Catalan, but families can choose to send their children to schools where Castilian is the first language of instruction. Fluent Catalan is required for city and regional government jobs.

It might help to decode all those "x's" if you pronounced them as "ch" or "sh," as in *anxoves* = anchovies. Accent marks show where emphasis falls.

the rebel troops of General Francisco Franco at the war's end in 1939.

During the Civil War some 700,000 men on both sides died on the battlefield, 30,000 were executed or assassinated, including many priests and nuns, and perhaps 15,000 civilians were killed in air raids. Barcelona was repeatedly bombed and its people suffered great hardships.

Catalonia paid a heavy price in defeat. All regional institutions were again abolished and controls from the central government were reimposed. The Catalan language was again proscribed, even in schools and churches. For years, Barcelona got little support from Madrid. Nevertheless, its industry recovered and a million or more job hunters from less prosperous parts of Spain migrated to the Barcelona area. From the 1960s a tourism boom lifted the economy and brought the people of conservative Franco Spain in touch with modern Europe, with Barcelona leading the way.

When Franco died in 1975, the country had already begun to emerge from its isolation. The coronation of his designated successor, Juan Carlos (Joan Carles to the Catalans), the grandson of Alfonso XIII, brought the restoration of parliamentary democracy and a revolutionary relaxation of customs and laws. In the 1978 Constitution, degrees of autonomy were granted to the fractious regions. While a militant Basque minority demanded more independence and resorted to terror tactics, most Catalans were content with the restoration of the Generalitat and regional parliament and the return of Catalan as an official language.

The freeing of controls within the European Union to create a single market finds Barcelona, Spain's industrial engine and bridge to the rest of Europe, poised for a boom and looking to the future with optimism.

HISTORICAL LANDMARKS

900 – 400 b.c.	Celtic tribes settle and mix with indigenous Iberians.
237 b.c.	Carthaginian general, Hamilcar Barca, establishes base at Barcino.
206 b.c.	Romans defeat Carthaginians.
1st c. a.d.	Christian settlements spread through Catalonia.
531–554	Barcelona capital of Visigoths.
711	Moorish invasion of Spain.
732	After defeat by Franks, Moors withdraw from Catalonia.
878	Wilfred the Hairy founds dynasty of counts of Barcelona.
1096–1131	Ramón Berenguer III extends Catalan empire.
1213–1276	Jaume I consolidates empire, expands Barcelona.
1283	Corts (Parliament) of Catalonia established.
1469	Marriage of Ferdinand and Isabella unites Aragón-Catalonia with Castile to create a unified Spain.
1494	Administration of Catalonia put under Castilian control.
1516	Charles I (Charles V, Holy Roman Emperor) takes throne.
1640	Catalonia declares itself a republic allied to France.
1652	Catalan territories north of Pyrenees ceded to France.
1701–1713	War of Spanish Succession.
1713–1714	Siege of Barcelona by Philip V; Ciutadella fortress built.
1808–1814	Peninsular War between English and Napoleon.
1835	Sequestration of church properties.
1870s	Renaissance of Catalan art.
1888	Universal Exposition in Barcelona.
1914	Mancomunitat formed in Catalonia.
1924	General Primo de Rivera sets up military dictatorship, bans Catalan language and dissolves Mancomunitat.
1929	International Exhibition in Barcelona.
1931	Republican party comes to power.
1932	Catalonia wins home rule.
1936 – 1939	Spanish Civil War ends in Franco dictatorship.
1975	Franco dies, Juan Carlos becomes king.
1980s	Catalonia achieves autonomy, Catalan language restored.
1986	Spain joins European Community (now European Union).
1992	Summer Olympics in Barcelona.

WHERE TO GO

Time, that's the problem. There's a lot to do and see in Barcelona, so planning your day is important. You set out with the best of intentions only to get sidetracked in the colourful maze of a covered market or a street of antiques shops. Then the sight of glistening shrimp on a bed of ice in the doorway of a bar proves irresistible. You sink into a chair at a sidewalk table for a snack, read a newspaper, and before you know it, a church bell strikes noon. Is it too late to "do" the museum you started out to see? Or too early to ride the aerial cable car across the harbour for lunch at La Barceloneta beach? Decisions, decisions! And what's that archway across the street? The courtyard beyond looks interesting. You step in for a peek and find a small gem of architecture. Be forewarned about Barcelona's seductions or you may miss some of its outstanding attractions.

> **Male waiters are called *camarero* (cahmah**ray**ro) female *camarera* (cahmah**ray**rah).**

Very broadly grouped, these are the Barri Gòtic and other medieval districts, the great art museums, spanning the Romanesque period to Picasso, the astonishing architectural fantasies of Antoni Gaudí and his contemporaries, and the Ramblas with their byways and tapas bars. We have divided Barcelona into easily manageable sections. In the old town, where many streets are too narrow for cars and where a slow pace is rewarded by so many hidden treasures, the best way to cover the ground is on foot.

Each section describing this area is organized in the order of a walking tour, but it is always possible to opt for a different route from the one proposed. For sights farther afield, Barcelona has an excellent public transport network—clean

Las Ramblas: the perfect place to take in the special Barcelona atmosphere.

and frequent metro trains, modern buses, funiculars, and cable cars—as well as plenty of inexpensive taxis. A good map is essential, but don't be fooled by how near things look on paper. It's a big city.

Las Ramblas

Start with the Ramblas and immerse yourself in the special Barcelona atmosphere—energetic, artistic, democratic, and indulgent. This broad, tree-shaded promenade stretches nearly 2 km (1 mile) down a gentle incline from the city's hub, the Plaça de Catalunya (see page 54), to the waterfront. Las Ramblas take their name not from the rambling pace of boulevardiers, but from an Arabic word meaning a sandy, dry river bed, which indeed they originally were. In the 13th century a wall ran alongside the gully with roads on each side, like the streets that today one has to dart across through traffic to reach the central walkway.

There are five sections to the Ramblas if you go by the street signs. Actually they merge seamlessly, though as you stroll along, the character and denizens of the Ramblas do change. The short **Rambla de Canaletes** at the top is where crowds pour in from the Plaça de Catalunya or come up from the metro and train stations beneath. On Sundays and Mondays in season you'll find knots of gesticulating fans replaying the games of the Barça, Barcelona's beloved football club. This is their recognized turf. Here, too, begin the stalls where you can buy not only foreign newspapers and magazines, often on the day of issue, but also books, for Barcelona is a centre of publishing. The farther down Las Ramblas you go, however, the more the publications reflect the relaxation of pornography laws.

The **Rambla dels Estudis** is popularly called the Rambla dels Ocells, "of the birds," because it narrows here to become an outdoor aviary where birds of all descriptions are sold. When the vendors leave, their stalls lined with cages are folded and shut like wardrobes, with the birds rustling about. Pigeons flaunt their liberty, scavenging fallen seed and circling over the prisons of their cousins.

Birds give way to blossoms in the Rambla de les Flors, officially the **Rambla de Sant Josep**, the very emblem of Barcelona to the world and probably the most photographed scene in the city. Two products of this Rambla enjoy a brisk trade on April 23, the day of Barcelona's patron, Sant Jordi (St. George), which is celebrated as the Day of the Book and when it is also traditional to give girls a rose. Facing the "Lane of Flowers" is the elegant **Palau de la Virreina**, a palace completed in 1778 for the widow of the viceroy of colonial Peru. At street level is a service of the city's Department of Culture, where tickets to municipal concerts are sold or offered and information about museums and current exhibitions is available.

Set back from the street, a giant red pepper stands under a stained-glass medallion hanging over the entrance to the overflowing cornucopia of earthly delights that is the Mercat de Sant Josep, or **La Boqueria**. This is the queen of Barcelona's many magnificent 19th-century covered markets. La Boqueria is a community where shoppers and merchants greet each other by name. where ribald sallies across the aisles set off gales of laughter, where the freshness of a *rape* (an angler fish popular in Catalonia) is debated with the passion of a traffic mishap.

The market is huge, laid out under high-ceilinged ironwork naves, like a railway station. And huge are the heaps of fruit, vegetables, seafood, sausages, meat and poultry, and enough spices, neatly braided ropes of garlic, sun-dried tomatoes and peppers, preserves, and sweetmeats to make a gourmet swoon.

A fire-juggler lights up the night for onlookers along Las Ramblas.

Restaurants in and near the market are like first-aid stations for those who become faint with hunger at the sight of such riches. The market opens before dawn, but closes down in mid-afternoon. The best time to visit is in the morning.

The heart of the Ramblas is the **Pla de la Boqueria.** The Rambla's busiest intersection broadens here at the market and at the staircase to a metro station. The centre of the pla ("square" or "plain" in Catalan) is paved with a mosaic unmistakably by Joan Miró. You'll be coming back again and again to this focal point, whether from walks in the Barri Gòtic, the Gothic quarter to the left (see pages 30–43), or from exploring El Raval, the district to the right (see pages

A "living statue" draws mixed reviews. Strollers expect the unexpected on Las Ramblas.

56–58). Here also remains the shell of one of Spain's great opera houses, the **Gran Teatre del Liceu**. A monument of the Catalan Renaixença (renaissance) opened in 1847, the Liceu suffered irreparable damage to its interior after a fire in January 1994. Only the front of the theatre is still intact. A project to rebuild this cultural monument is underway and will include many technical improvements, one of which will be equipment for television broadcast.

The secret of Catalan cooking is the freshness of its produce, spread in a carpet of colour at markets like La Boqueria.

Across the way is the venerable **Café del'Opera**, a good spot for a bit of refreshment before you push on down the next stretch, the **Rambla dels Caputxins**. The tone and the incline are both a bit downhill after the Liceu, but the street entertainment starts here. You'll encounter jugglers, fire-eaters, sidewalk artists, including those reproducing masterworks in chalks on the pavement, tarot-card readers, "human statues," violinists, lottery-ticket sellers, assorted crack-pots, and mendicants.

Note the naïve painted angels floating over the doorway of the old **Hotel**

Oriente, which preserves part of the 17th-century cloister of a Franciscan school inside. Just beyond the hotel on the Carrer Nou de la Rambla, is the **Palau Güell**, the mansion Gaudí (see page 51) built in 1885 for his principal patron, the textile tycoon Count Eusebi Güell. A brief detour from the Rambla is in order to see this meticulously detailed fortress-like home, now a theatrical museum.

Returning to the Ramblas, cross over and follow the short passage that leads into the arcaded **Plaça Reial**. This handsome and spacious square is graced with a fountain, palm trees, and wrought-iron lampposts by the young Gaudí. Like the Boqueria, the Hotel Oriente, and other Rambla landmarks, this square came into being as a result of the destruction of a convent when church properties were expropriated in an anti-clerical period in the mid-19th century. Today it is somewhat decayed, best known for its cafés and for a stamp and coin market held on Sunday mornings.

> **Underground fare in Barcelona is the same irrespective of the distance you travel.**

The final promenade leading to the harbour is the short **Rambla de Santa Mònica**, beginning at the Plaça del Teatre, site of the run-down **Teatre Principal**. The area is the beat of prostitutes and cops on the lookout for pickpockets and bag-snatchers. The warren of alleys to the right is the Barri Xino, or Chinatown, once notorious for forbidden sin. With the new openness of the post-Franco era it has lost much of its interest, but it's still no place for a midnight stroll.

The **Carrer dels Escudellers** on the other side of the Rambla is the gateway to a district of cabarets, bars, flamenco shows, and restaurants, including the well-known Los Caracoles, where chickens are turned on spits on the street corner.

Nearer the port, a passage leads to the **Museu de Cera** (Wax Museum), with its collection of around three hundred realistic wax effigies. The Rambla ends at the broad open space of the **Plaça del Portal de la Pau** (Gate of Peace Square) and the Monument a Colom, in honour of Columbus (Colom in Catalan). This is also the starting point for walks along the waterfront (see pages 58–63).

Barri Gòtic

Barcelona has grown outwards in rings from its beginnings more than two thousand years ago, like concentric ripples on a pond. The ancient core is a hill the Romans called Mons Taber where they raised a temple to Augustus Caesar, and in the fourth century built high walls about a mile around to protect their settlement. The Visigoths and Frankish rulers who followed also lived within the first ring, the nucleus of the medieval district called the Barri Gòtic. In the 1940s the clutter of buildings that over the centuries had encrusted this centre like barnacles on a ship were removed. The best were dismantled and relocated. The walls and main palaces were thus restored to view and the district has become the main attraction for visitors, as well as a lively centre of administration, commerce, and art for Barcelona.

Taking off again from the Plaça de Catalunya, follow the Avinguda del Portal de l'Àngel past El Corte Inglés department store to the **Col.legi d'Arquitectes** (College of Architects). The full-stop in Col.legi is a Catalan punctuation that indicates a stretching of the "L" sound. Picasso contributed the drawings of the Three Kings and the children bearing palm branches engraved on the modern façade. The theme perhaps alludes to the street market that sells Christ-

Street artist depicts a heavenly scene at Plaça de Catalunya.

mas crib figurines from December 6–24 around the corner in the **Plaça Nova**—a square that got its name, meaning "new," in 1356. This open space has held markets for nearly a thousand years. These days antiques dealers set up stalls every Thursday in front of the steps by the towers of the Roman wall.

To get the mood of the old fortified core, follow the walls for a bit, passing in front of the cathedral, and continue along the Carrer de la Tapineria. This leads to the **Plaça de Berenguer el Gran**, whose statue on horseback seems small beside the well-preserved section of wall at this point. The Roman defences are 9 metres (30 feet) high and 3.5 metres (11.8 feet) thick and were marked at intervals by towers 18 metres (59 feet) tall. Until 1943, most of this section was covered by a clutter of old houses, which were dismantled and relocated to restore the walls and old mansions to view.

The Baixada de la Llibreteria crosses the wall line into the Barri Gòtic, and the first turning to the right leads immediately to the **Museu d'Història de la Ciutat** (Museum of History of the City). The building is a Gothic mansion that was moved stone by stone to this location. Its exhibits are worth visiting early in your stay to get your bearings and some historical perspective.

Signs:
entrada-entrance
salida - exit
llegada - arrival
salida - departure
rebajas - sale
fumadores - smoker
no fumadores - nonsmoker

Go first to the basement, where excavations have uncovered sculptures, streets, house walls, a bathing pool, drains, and cemeteries of the Roman and even pre-Roman Mons Taber. Then proceed to the upper floors, where you'll see maps of the Catalan empire at its height, with consulates all around the Mediterranean, from

Tripoli to Tyre. Another series of maps and engravings shows the 1713–1714 siege of Barcelona by Philip V, demonstrating how the walls were breached. A flag of the Guild of Gardeners emblazoned with pruning knives, hoes, and other humble tools, a collection of tiles illustrating medieval occupations, and a family tree of trades are marks of the respect for business that has characterized Barcelona from its beginnings and are also evidence of the prestige of the craft guilds in the Middle Ages. A huge iron-and-wood clockworks on display, made in 1575, weighs 5,512 kilograms (12,152 pounds). It told the time and rang the cathedral bells for three hundred years. Here too are the original plans for the 19th-century expansion of the city that created the Eixample district beyond the old walls.

From the museum it is a step to the Plaça del Rei, the courtyard of the **Palau Reial** (Royal Palace), dominated by the many-arched lookout tower of King Martin and, atop the Roman walls, the **Capella de Santa Àgata** (Chapel of St. Agatha). The chapel is notable for the 15th-century altarpiece of the *Adoration of the Magi* by one of Catalonia's finest artists, Jaume Huguet. St. Agatha was martyred by having her breasts cut off. A curious painting shows the unruffled saint holding them on a plate.

In the courtyard, the structure with the broad staircase is all that is left of the original Royal Palace of Catalonia, begun in the tenth century and added to over the years until it took up three sides of the square and extended to the rear. During the Inquisition, suspected heretics were burned at the stake in this enclosure, and here Ferdinand and Isabella received Columbus on his return from his first voyage in 1493.

Columbus probably gave his report in the **Saló del Tinell**. This vast barrel-vaulted hall was built for royal audiences in 1359, and on occasion the Catalan Corts (Parliament) met here. The walls were once decorated with murals, a fragment of which is preserved in the city museum.

The palace's central section, chapel, and hall were reconstructed between 1943 and 1952. Outdoor theatre and concerts are held in the square in summer. It looks its best at night, with lights picking out the arches and the half-darkness giving imagination full rein.

A former wing of the palace which encloses the Plaça del Rei was rebuilt in 1557 to become the **Palau del Lloctinent** (Palace of the Lieutenant), residence of the king's representative. It now houses the Archives of Aragón. The entrance, reached by leaving the palace square and turning right on the Carrer dels Comtes, is an elegant patio with a noble staircase and remarkable carved wooden ceiling. The intriguing bronze door on the staircase is by the modern Barcelona artist Nùria Fedra. A few steps farther on is the tiny Plaça de Sant Iu, adorned with the Renaissance doorway that once stood at the top of the Royal Palace stairs. Down a few steps is a courtyard with benches amid bits and pieces of ruins and the entrance to the **Museu Frederic Marés**.

Frederic Marés was a competent 20th-century sculptor of civic statues, but he will be best remembered as a compulsive collector who gave Barcelona one of the most idiosyncratic, magpie collections of art and miscellany ever brought under one roof. The lower floors of the museum are notable for Iberian votive figurines, Limoges enamel boxes, the Romanesque portal of a church from Huesca, and a sampling of religious sculptures from the 12th to 19th centuries. Among exhibits on the second floor is a lovely 15th-century painted English *Virgen de la Misericordia*. Farther upstairs, the collection changes abruptly. Portuguese carved and painted ox yokes, a roomful of iron keys, old sewing machines, stereopticon views, canes, lead soldiers, wind-up toys. . . the catalogue is endless. There is even the suitcase, covered with travel stickers, in which Marés brought home his loot.

Retracing your steps on the narrow street flanking the cathedral, circle around it to the rear and duck into the narrow Carrer del Paradís. Here, just inside the doorway of the **Centre Excursionista de Catalunya**, four columns of the Roman Temple of Augustus are embedded in the wall.

Behind the cathedral apse, in the Carrer de la Pietat, stands a good example of a 14th-century Catalan house, the **Casa dels Canonges**. This former chapter house of the cathedral canons was restored in 1929 for official use. Next comes a small open space where musicians, like the troubadours of old, play for contributions beside the Flamboyant Gothic **Porta de la Pietat** cathedral door noted for a Flemish carved wooden panel above its lintel.

Here the street leads into the Carrer del Bisbe Irurita which in turn brings you to the Carrer de Santa Llúcia. To the left is the **Palau Episcopal**, the 18th-century Baroque Bishop's Palace, with an austere courtyard. The more appealing **Casa de l'Ardiaca**, once the archdeacon's residence, has a curious marble letterbox panel of swallows and a tortoise, a 19th-century contribution of the modernist architect Domènech i Montaner. Inside, an informal patio is decorated with brightly coloured floral tiles.

And now you finally approach the front of the **Catedral de la Santa Cruz y Santa Eulàlia**. The platform between its portico and the steps leading down to the Plaça Nova and the Avinguda de la Catedral is the Pla de la Seu, where impromptu dancing of the *sardana* takes place on Sundays and holidays. The Gothic buildings on the far side of the steps have been restored. Where a hundred poor persons a day were once fed at a medieval almshouse there are now souvenir shops.

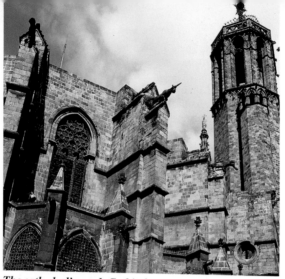

The cathedral's mock-Gothic façade was added in 1892.

The cathedral was begun in 1298 on the site of earlier churches going back to Visigothic times. The final touch, the rather florid Gothic façade, not completed until 1892, contrasts with the simple octagonal towers. The cathedral's cool, dark interior and leafy cloister offer welcome relief from the heat of a summer's day. The ribs of the high vault are joined at carved and painted keystone medallions, a typically Catalan feature. In the centre of the nave is a Gothic choir with lacy spires of carved wood over each seat. Above these are the heraldic emblems of the European kings and princes invited by Charles V to be members of his exclusive Order of the Golden Fleece *(Toison d'Or)*. The first and only meeting was held in the cathedral in 1519. The seats reserved for Henry VIII of England and

François I of France are next to the emperor's, but they did not show up.

Connected to the choir is a pulpit with an exceptional wrought-iron stair rail. Ahead, steps under the altar lead to the alabaster tomb of Santa Eulàlia, one of the city's two patron saints, martyred in the fourth century. Notice the angel choir of plump stone heads around the stairway and crypt arch—actually portraits of royalty who attended the transfer of her remains here in 1339. On the wall of the right aisle are the tombs of Count Ramón Berenguer I and his wife Almodis, who founded the earlier cathedral on this spot in 1058—both of them very short, it seems. Don't miss the Catalan Gothic altarpieces in the chapels behind the altar. The nine panels of the Transfiguration painted for the San Benito chapel in the 15th century by Bernat Martorell are considered his masterpiece.

The **cloister** is a-twitter with birds fluttering in the orange, magnolia, and palm trees that entirely fill its centre. The cloister is paved with tombstones, badly worn, but many still bearing the emblems of the bootmakers, tailors, and other craft guilds whose wealth helped pay for the cathedral. One chapel is dedicated to 930 priests and nuns of the diocese killed in the anti-clerical slaughter of the 1936–1939 Civil War. From the cloister, pass to the **Capella de Santa Llúcia** (Chapel of St. Lucy), with 13th- and 14th-century tombstones on the floor and the monument to a crusader knight in armour on a wall.

Leaving the Capella de Santa Llúcia by its front entrance, turn left at the Carrer del Bisbe Irurita. The corner house at Number 8 was the official residence of the president of the Generalitat until recently. Keep looking upwards as you walk through the old town. There's always something interesting to see: a curious hanging sign or

Raw realism and roses: two sides of faith in the cathedral cloister.

lantern or an unusual sculpture. Here on the right you'll find a row of gargoyles leaning from the roof of the Palau de la Generalitat, the seat of government for the Autonomous Region of Catalonia, and a richly ornamented gateway. Above it is a medallion with Sant Jordi (St. George) on a kind of merry-go-round horse. The lacy overhead bridge is a 1929 addition that fits in well.

Back down Carrer del Bisbe Irurita you emerge into the spacious **Plaça de Sant Jaume**, the heart of the Barri Gòtic. A local joke says that the farthest distance in Barcelona is across this square, which separates the often antagonistic Generalitat from the municipal authorities in the Ajuntament, the City Hall. Together they must haggle with Madrid, for the central government collects the main taxes, returning a share to the region. Then a further slicing of the pie and decisions on who pays for what bring confrontations between the socialist authorities of Barcelona and the more conservative regional authority. Architecturally the two buildings make a harmonious pair. Both have classical façades that hide their Gothic origins.

The **Palau de la Generalitat** is the more interesting of the two. This institution dates from 1359, when it was made the executive branch reporting to the parliament, the Corts of Catalonia. The nucleus of the present building is the main patio of purest Catalan Gothic, with its open staircase leading to a gallery of arches on slender pillars. In 1526 the unusual upper patio was added. It is planted with orange trees whose perfume undermines the bureaucratic atmosphere in spring. The jewel of the building is the sumptuous Flamboyant Gothic façade of the **Capella de Sant Jordi**. You can't get away from St. George here. The **Saló de Sant Jordi**, a large vaulted hall in the 17th-century front block of the building, is lined with modern murals of historical scenes. In the past, the palace has indeed had its ups and downs. The Generalitat was abolished in 1714 by Philip V, who made the building a court. This it remained until 1908, when it became the seat of the crown's provincial authorities until the brief period of autonomy under the 1931–1939 Republic. A provincial office again during the Franco years, it finally welcomed back the revived Generalitat in 1977.

The **Ajuntament**, or Casa de la Ciutat, across the way has been Barcelona's city hall since 1372. It was here that the Consell de Cent, a council of 100 notable citizens, met to deal with civic affairs under the watchful eyes of the king. The original entrance can be seen around the left-hand corner of the building, on the Carrer de la Ciutat. The very official-looking new façade was erected in 1845. Inside, the left staircase leads to the upper gallery of the old courtyard and to the **Saló de Cent** (Hall of the One Hundred). Its high ceiling resembles the barrel-vault of the Saló del Tinell, and was built at about the same time in the 14th century. The red-and-yellow bars of Catalonia's flag decorate the walls. The hall where the city council now meets adjoins, and at the head of the black marble staircase is the **Saló de les Cròniques** (Hall of the Chronicles), noted for the modern murals in sepia tones by Josep Maria Sert. The fellow with the knife in his back is Roger de Flor, the Catalan corsair who was assassinated during the campaign depicted here when his mercenaries took Athens.

From behind the Ajuntament, take the short Carrer d'Hèrcules to the **Plaça de Sant Just** for a look at the church of **Sants Just i Pastor**. The small square is enough off the beaten track and lacking in "improvements" to preserve the flavour of a bygone Barcelona. There's a fountain installed in 1367 that is still in use (with new fixtures). The church is one of the oldest in the city, though often remodelled. Since the tenth century any will sworn to before the church's altar is recognized as valid by the courts of Barcelona.

Since ancient times, when two main Roman thoroughfares intersected here, the Plaça de Sant Jaume has been the crossroads of Barcelona. Streets radiate in all directions, each an invitation to explore the Barri Gòtic. The Carrer del Call leads into the labyrinth of narrow streets that was the **Call**, or Jewish Quarter, until the Jews were expelled in 1492. Today the quarter is almost solid antiques shops and dealers in rare books, plus bars and restaurants frequented by antiquarians and artists.

Although many of the streets have Call in their names, there are few vestiges left of the ghetto, which once was surrounded by a wall. The Jews of Barcelona, though noted as doctors, scholars, and jewellers, and despite their financing of the conquests of the crown, were confined to this district and had to wear long-hooded cloaks with a yellow headband. Taxes on Jews were a special source of royal income. This did not, however, save the Call from being burned and looted as persecution mounted in the 14th and 15th centuries. Stones from Jewish tombs can be seen in the west wall of the Generalitat and other Barri Gòtic palaces, and just off the Carrer del Call, at Number 1 Carrer de Marlet, a medieval inscription in Hebrew marks the site of a hospital founded by one "Rabbi Samuel Hassareri, may his life never cease."

Farther on is the Baixada de Santa Eulàlia. Local lore holds that the saint was martyred here in 304 by being rolled down the slope in a barrel full of broken glass, though the official record has her done in far across the country, in Mérida. A few steps more bring one into a tiny square closed to traffic where kids love to play football. This is the **Plaça de Sant Felip Neri**. The saint's church was pockmarked by Italian bombs during the Civil War. To the right are two houses of medieval guilds, first the **Casa dels Calderers** (House of the Cauldron-Makers), and then the **Casa Gremial dels Sabaters** (House of the Shoemakers), which contains a small museum of footwear, including some high-button shoes of Pau (Pablo) Casals. Both buildings were moved here during the construction of streets that opened up the Barri Gòtic beyond the cathedral.

The Baixada de Santa Eulàlia descends to the **Carrer dels Banys Nous**, named for the long-gone "new" baths of the ghetto erected in the 12th century. This curving street more or less follows the line of the old Roman wall and is the unofficial boundary of the Barri Gòtic. Keep your eyes peeled as you walk along for odd handpainted shop signs, the fretwork of Gothic windows, and treasures (or reasonable facsimiles) in the antiques shop windows. You'll see the old tile signs with a cart symbol high in the walls at some corners, the indication of one-way streets. Within the walls in the 19th century, Barcelona had more than 200 streets less than 3 metres (10 feet) wide.

Forge ahead into the Plaça de Sant Josep Oriol, which connects with the Plaça del Pi in front of **Santa Maria del Pi**, a handsome church with a tall octagonal bell tower and a harmonious façade pierced by a large rose window completed in 1453. "Pi" means pine tree, and there is a small specimen here replacing one that was a landmark in past centuries. The two adjoining squares, together with the small Placeta del Pi to the rear of the church, are the essence of old Barcelona.

All around, a shifting cast of characters—musicians, puppeteers, pantomimists, hawkers of handicrafts, and panhandlers—vie for attention. Shopkeepers gossip on the doorsteps of once-important buildings whose walls are adorned with allegorical figures in *esgrafiado*, the *sgrafitto* technique of scraping designs in coloured plaster, imported from Italy in the early 1700s. (The up-and-coming Barcelona merchant class favoured such façades as an inexpensive substitute for the sculpture found in aristocratic palaces.) A bar with tables under spreading plane trees is a shady oasis by day and equally popular by night, when the church and square are lit up. On Sundays, artists offer their canvases for sale here, and a large arcade of shops sells a miscellany of trendy goods.

One other tranquil and beautiful corner should be visited before leaving this part of the city, the **Monestir de Santa Anna**. The Carrer de Santa Anna is off the commercial Avinguda del Portal de l'Angel and it, too, is crowded with shoppers. Through a dark archway an open space with trees and benches beckons. The simple lines of a low Romanesque church contrast with the backs of tall office build-

On Sundays artists offer their canvases for sale on the Plaça del Pi, otherwise crowded with a curious cast of characters

ings just beyond. In the 11th century, the monastery stood in fields outside the Roman walls. All that's left now is a small cloister and the church, a little island of calm.

Santa Maria del Mar

Some of the most beautiful Gothic architecture and most fascinating medieval corners of Barcelona lie outside the Barri Gòtic. To the east of the Via Laietana—a busy avenue roughly parallel to the Ramblas cut through the old city in 1909 to link the port with the modern centre—and below the Carrer de la Princesa, which intersects it at midpoint, is the atmospheric quarter centred on the majestic church of **Santa Maria del Mar** (St. Mary of the Sea).

Santa Maria del Mar's simple lines are purest Catalan Gothic.

The Carrer Argenteria, once the avenue to the sea from the Royal Palace, leads to the church from the Plaça de l'Angel. Begun in 1329 at the height of Catalonia's expansion as a Mediterranean power, Santa Maria del Mar is pure Catalan Gothic, with unadorned exterior walls, a flat roof, sober façade flanked by two three-tiered octagonal bell towers, and a large rose window over the portal.

Fires set alight in the rioting of 1936 at the outbreak of the Civil War tragically consumed all the trappings of chapels, choir, and altar, leaving the interior stripped to its essence.

The result is a spacious and lofty hall suffused with soft light from the stained-glass windows. Three tall naves are supported by slim octagonal columns set 13 metres (43 feet) apart, and the dimensions of the interior are multiples of this distance, achieving a perfect symmetry.

Behind the simple modern altar, the columns branch high overhead into the arched vaulting of the apse. The acoustics are excellent for the concerts often held in the church and for the voices of choirboys at mass.

The rear door of the church leads to the **Passeig del Born**, a large open space where jousts were held in the Middle Ages and fairs and festivals take place today. Many of the little streets surrounding the church are named after the craftsmen who once had their shops here, or after their products, such as Sombrerers (Hatters), Mirallers (Mirror-makers), Esparteria (Makers of rope-soled shoes), and Espaseria (Sword-makers).

Ducking down these alleys leads one back through centuries. The **Carrer de les Caputxes** (Hoods) in front of the church is one of the least changed by time. In the short **Carrer del Fossar de les Moreres**, a plaque marks the common grave of men who fell defending the city during the 1713–1714 siege of the city.

The **Carrer de les Mosques** (*Mosques* means flies) behind the Born on the other side of the church is less than 1.5 metres (5 feet) wide, the city's narrowest.

Off the Born in the little Plaça de les Olles down the Carrer de la Vidrieria (Glassmakers) is a pastry shop founded in 1878, where you can watch goodies being made in a window and then go inside and see if they taste as delicious as they look. At the end of the Passeig del Born is the large iron and glass shed of **El Born**, the former wholesale market now used for theatrical and musical spectacles.

Nearby is the **Homage to Picasso** by Spain's leading abstract artist, Antoni Tàpies. It's a 4-metre (13-feet) glass cube set in a pool of rushing water. A screen of water running down the inner walls of the cube distorts and makes mysterious the contents—iron rods, and a sofa and chair covered by a dust cloth, as if shut up in an empty house.

Picasso's own museum is reached from the Born by the **Carrer de Montcada**, a street populated by aristocrats from the 14th to the 16th centuries. It is lined with palaces, each with an imposing door or arched gate to an inner court where an ornamental staircase usually led up to reception rooms. These mansions were gradually abandoned after the demolition of the adjoining district and construction of the Ciutadella fortress. Then the business of the port moved closer to the Ramblas, and the new centre of fashion became the Carrer Ample and the church of La Mercè. The quarter around Santa Maria del Mar decayed gently without interference, leaving it the most authentically medieval part of the city.

Today the area is enjoying a revival as a neighbourhood of art galleries around the **Museu Picasso**. The Palau Aguilar, a 15th-century mansion, was acquired by the city to house, along with the Palau Castellet, the collection of paintings, drawings, and ceramics donated by Picasso's lifelong friend and secretary, Jaume Sabartés. After the museum opened in 1963, Picasso added sketches and paintings from his childhood and youth, as well as the famous 44 variations on the theme of *Las Meninas*, the Velázquez masterpiece in Madrid's Prado Museum.

The earliest items date from Picasso's ninth year. Before long he was doing very creditable sketches of his father, mother, and sister. And as a teenager he produced large canvases in the moralizing 19th-century realist manner, such as the *First*

Splendid Renaissance palaces, complete with ornamental staircases, line the Carrer de Montcada.

Communion and *Science and Charity*. There follow the sketchbooks from his first visits to Paris and the results of his exposure to the styles of Toulouse-Lautrec, Renoir, and others.

As he develops, it is as if he digested the styles of the past and of his contemporaries, proved he could match them, then forged energetically ahead into the future. He is his own man with two good examples of the "Blue Period" (1903) and with the *The Harlequin* (1917). The museum does not attempt to document each phase of the painter's extraordinary career.

The rooms exhibiting the *Las Meninas* series give a fascinating view of Picasso's approach to his subject, taking it apart, emphasizing now this, now that element. In one version, he brings Velázquez out of the shadowy background of the original and has him dominating his picture. Finally, there are rooms dedicated to drawings and lithographs. The last is dated 1972, the year before his death, showing the Picasso line as bold and sure as ever. The museum is open daily from 10:00 A.M. to 8:00 P.M., and is closed on Mondays. There is a stone-vaulted coffee bar off the patio of the building.

Across the street is the **Museu Tèxtil i de la Indumentària** (Textile and Costume Museum) in the former palace of the Marquesos de Lló. It's a very handsome residence, and its collection brings to life the elegance enjoyed by the rich families who occupied such houses. The costumes exhibited are of superb silks, satins, and furs, embroidered and stitched to perfection. Styles represented come right down to flapper dresses of the 1920s. The museum is open daily from 9:00 A.M. to 2:00 P.M. and 4:30 to 7:00 P.M. and is closed on Mondays.

The Carrer de la Princesa leads back to the centre of things and the Via Laietana. Above this street are other points of interest, such as the tiny Romanesque **Capella de Marcús** on the continuation of Carrer de Montcada, and around the corner from it, on the Carrer dels Carders, the picturesque courtyard of the **Hostal de la Bona Sort**, or "Good Luck Lodge," once an inn for carters. The heart of this quarter is the **Mercat de Santa Caterina**, a large market square in a typically Barcelonan neighbourhood.

L'Eixample

The modern centre of Barcelona is called the "Eixample" in Catalan and the "Ensanche" in Spanish, meaning the Expansion district. It came about all at once in a remarkable burst of urban development that also made the city the showcase of Modernisme in the extravagant architecture of Antoni

Gaudí and his peers. By the mid-1800s Barcelona was bursting at the seams and suffocating inside its ring of medieval walls. A competition was held in 1859 to select a plan for a new quarter between the old city and the Collserola hills. After some dispute the job went to a road engineer named Ildefons Cerdà. His plan quintupled the city's size in a matter of decades. It called for a grid of streets with the corners of the blocks cut off to make every intersection spacious. He proposed that construction be on three sides only of each block, leaving the centre and one side for gardens.

Several broad avenues connecting major plazas were laid out on his grid—the Gran Via de les Corts Catalanes, or Gran Via, parallel to the sea, and the Passeig de Gràcia, perpendicular to it. A long boulevard, the Avinguda Diagonal (see pages 79–80), cut across the new district from the coast to the hills. The central points were to be the new Plaça de

Picasso

Pablo (Pau) Ruiz y Picasso was born in 1881 in Málaga, the son of a drawing teacher whose work took the family to Barcelona, where Picasso demonstrated precocious artistic skill. In 1900 he visited Paris, and settled there four years later. Picasso never returned to Barcelona after 1934, and in any case his opposition to the Franco regime would have made this impossible. When Picasso died in 1973 the bulk of his own collection, now in the Musée Picasso in Paris, went to the French government in a deal to settle taxes.

Barcelona's Picassos are nevertheless extremely interesting. It is almost unbelievable that the painter of the saccharine but technically impeccable *First Communion* was a 15-year-old, or that the vigorous lines of the sprawling nudes dated 1972 were the work of a nonagenarian, and that Picasso created both.

Catalunya, between the head of the Ramblas and the Passeig de Gràcia, and the Plaça d'Espanya and the Plaça de les Glòries Catalanes on the Gran Via between Montjuïc and the Diagonal.

Tearing down the walls was like removing a corset; Barcelona could breathe. Construction went ahead at a fast pace. The rich and the middling rich moved into the new district and built large homes. The notion of gardens within the blocks was quickly abandoned, land being too valuable. The Passeig de Gràcia became the place to be seen. The moment coincided with the 1888 Universal Exposition, Barcelona's open house to show the world its new face, and with a European vogue in design for what the French called Art Nouveau, the Germans and Austrians called Jugendstil, and the Spanish dubbed Modernisme. It was a rebellion against the rigid forms and colourless stone and plaster of the Classical architecture that had replaced Gothic. Nowhere did this style thrive and take on nationalist motifs and meaning as in Barcelona, and nowhere has it been so carefully preserved.

Antoni Gaudí and Barcelona have become synonymous. The eccentric genius lived a long, productive life and his handiwork is found all over the city. But others excelled in the new style, too, notably Lluís Domènech i Montaner (1850–1923), creator of the astonishing Palau de la Música Catalana (see pages 54–56), and Josep Puig i Cadafalch (1867–1957), responsible for the turreted Casa de les Punxes on the Diagonal and Els Quatre Gats, the artists café at Number 3 Carrer Montsió. Both were prominent in the politics of Catalonia.

Houses of all three are found in one block called the "Block of Discord" on the west side of the Passeig de Gràcia between the Carrer del Consell de Cent and Carrer d'Aragó. (In Catalan the word for "apple" and "block" are the same— *mançana*—allowing this play on words alluding to the apple in Greek mythology awarded to the most beautiful among three goddesses, a contest that led inevitably to trouble.)

The first house, at Number 35, is the **Casa Lleó Morera** (1905), by Domènech i Montaner. It incorporates Moorish and Gothic elements, as well as decorations using recent inventions: the telephone, camera, and light bulb. The main floor is now occupied by the Barcelona Tourist Department,

Gaudí

No individual has left so personal a mark on a city as Antoni Gaudí on Barcelona. His style is so much his own that he has not been the fount of a continuing school and now seems to have been the only one of his kind. Looking back, one wonders how he convinced conservative merchants and churchmen to accept his far-out ideas. Count Eusebi Güell, a textile manufacturer, was his patient patron.

The Palau Güell, which Gaudí began in 1885, previews many aspects of Gaudí's work, in that it draws on styles of the past—Gothic and Moorish—and distorts them as a dream distorts reality. He was a talented designer of furniture and interior decorations and closely supervised every detail of the assignments he gave his artisans. The Sagrada Família gave scope to these trends (see pages 80–83).

For all his innovations, Gaudí was no Bohemian, but deeply religious and conservative in his own lifestyle. He had a sense of humour, too. When a client complained that there was no room for her piano in the music room he designed, Gaudí's response was "let her take up the violin." The architect died in 1926, hit by a tram. The hospital did not immediately identify the old man with a white beard, but when they did, the whole city turned out for his funeral.

so visitors can at least get a peek at the interior, richly decorated with carvings, mosaics, and stained glass. In the **Casa Amatller** (1900) at Number 41, Puig i Cadafalch drew inspiration from the Flemish for his stepped roof faced with glazed tiles. The Institut Amatller d'Art Hispànic here has furniture by the architect.

The Gaudí house, the **Casa Batlló** (1904), is next door. It is in an extreme personal style that immediately sets Gaudí apart from the others. The curvy contours, unexpected combinations of textures and materials, bright colours, and infinite detail are Gaudí hallmarks. Very often religious or nationalist symbolism is present. The Casa Batlló, for example, is said to symbolize Catalonia's patron, St. George, and the dragon. Gaudí left no clues on the matter. The blue-tile roof with orange knobs could be the dragon's scaly back and the window balconies the skulls and bones of its victims, while St. George's cross and a shaft suggesting a spear stab down from above. The façade is covered with the bits of broken plate and tile surfacing that he introduced, and with blue disks that are like bubbles rising in water.

Number 92, farther up and across the street, is the **Casa Milà**, known as La Pedrera, a Gaudí apartment house of 1905 that is classified by UNESCO as an artistic World Heritage Site. Tours of the building are conducted by the Fundació Caixa de Catalunya, but need to be booked well in advance (tel. 484 59 80). The sinuous façade with wrought-iron balconies that have been likened to seaweed is topped by a cluster of fanciful chimneys of swirling shapes that have mask-like apertures. Note the detail of carved doors (even the doorknobs are handcrafted), cobweb window frames, and metal ribbon patterns on bannisters. Gaudí gave the building one of the world's first underground parking garages.

Gaudí's Casa Milà, classified as an artistic World Heritage Site by UNESCO, is truly a sight to behold.

Outside you'll be walking on the pink and turquoise hexagonal tiles he designed for the pavements of the Passeig de Gràcia. The mosaic benches and iron street lamps with little bats (1900) are by Pere Falqués. Executing the intricate designs of the Modernist architects involved batteries of skilled cabinet makers, masons, iron workers, and artists in glass and ceramics. You'll find more examples of this unique style by other architects of the period in the streets crossing the Passeig de Gràcia to the east, such as Diputació, Consell de Cent, Mallorca, and València as far as the Mercat de la Concepció market. In the old town are marvellous Modernist store fronts, such as the Filatèlia Monge stamp shop at Carrer dels Boters 2, and the Antiga Casa Figueras bakery on the Ramblas. For details of tours of Modernist Barcelona see page 114.

The **Passeig de Gràcia** is a favourite street for strolling. There are outdoor cafés, cinemas, galleries combining many shops in one arcade, bookstores, quality leather goods, and fashion boutiques. Some of the top hotels are on or near this avenue. The **Plaça de Catalunya**, where it begins, was designed to be the city's hub. The bus, metro, and regional train systems radiate from this square. Unfortunately it is too big and too empty, despite encircling trees and robust 19th-century statues. It comes to life when the city stages rock concerts and other events in the central plaza. On Saturdays from 10:30 A.M. to 1:30 P.M., February to June, mothers bring their children here for free lessons in dancing the *sardana*. If you wish to watch a small rental fee will be charged for the chair.

An extension of the old Ramblas, the **Rambla de Catalunya** also climbs the slope here, parallel with the Passeig de Gràcia. Check the Sala Cultural of the Caja de Ahorros de Madrid savings bank on the corner for announcements of free concerts and lectures. The Rambla de Catalunya has a central walkway between Carrer de la Diputació and the Diagonal. More cinemas, boutiques, and bars, more banks, hotels, pastry shops (Mauri at the corner of Carrer de Provença is rather special), and more of the fast-food shops that are encroaching on the tapas bars in midtown. Two blocks west of this Rambla on the Gran Via is the old university centre at the Plaça de la Universitat.

☛ Palau de la Música Catalana

Gaudí's monuments are the most original, but the perfect expression of Modernisme is Lluís Domènech i Montaner's Palau de la Música Catalana. This peacock of a building is more decorated than the Tatooed Lady. No surface is left bare of its bit of mosaic, tile, stained glass, enamel, sculpture, or carving; no angle of vision is free from the tumultuous assault of contours and colours. The brick exterior is overpoweringly worked with Moorish arches, columns inlaid with floral designs in tile, stone roses, and what looks like a giant Easter egg swelling over a large

The wide-open Plaça de Catalunya was designed to be the hub of Barcelona.

mosaic of singers, and the Catalan flag. In the midst of all this, formal busts of Beethoven & Co. on the façade all look a bit disconcerted.

The best way to see the Palau is to attend a concert. The hall was built in 1908 for a musical society called the Orfeó Català. Its programmes feature top symphony orchestras and soloists. Tickets may be had during the season, October to June, at the box office on the Carrer Sant Pere més Alt near the top of Via Laietana. Guided tours can be booked in advance (tel. 268 10 00).

The exterior is sober compared to what's inside. Once again, every inch is embellished down to the tiles underfoot. The hall is nevertheless light and roomy. There are three tiers of seating and, because the structural skeleton is of iron—an innovation in those days—the walls, not needed for support, are free to be glass. It is stained of course. Sunlight at afternoon concerts supplements the rings of lights hanging at an angle from crown-like chandeliers. On either side of the orchestra's stage the rich colours of the room are offset by two wildly sculpted groups in white plaster. Between these fevered creations of the sculptor Pau Gargallo, Picasso's friend, the silvery pipes of a grand organ stand in orderly contrast.

Overhead is the Palau's crowning glory, a ceiling of stained glass that is at once a hanging bowl and an orb of golden discs that radiate flames towards segmented rings of angel faces. The level of boxes is open, the chairs enclosed by a curving rail of wood in front of the tall windows. There's no traditional red plush and gilt here, but pastel tones of rose, green, and amber. Behind the musicians a curving wall is covered with mosaics of muses playing instruments, from bagpipes to castanets. Magically, the upper part of their bodies is porcelain and seems to emerge from the walls. The whole thing verges on the chaotic, but is nevertheless marvellous.

El Raval

The district between the Ramblas and the Ronda de Sant Antoni, once the line of the city wall, is El Raval, a neighbourhood that has been recently renovated, with many old buildings demolished to create open spaces.

The best way to find the historic buildings is to start on the Ramblas, turning west on the Carrer del Carme or walking through the Boqueria market. At the corner of the market's parking lot is **Jardins Doctor Fleming**, the little square dedicated to the discoverer of penicillin.

Rejoin the Carrer del Carme here and turn into the Gothic complex of the **Hospital de la Santa Creu** (Hospital of the Holy Cross). A hospital and refuge for pilgrims stood on this spot for a thousand years. Gaudí died here in 1926, shortly before the medical establishment was moved across the Diagonal to new quarters designed by Domènech i Montaner.

The present structures were begun in 1401. At the left of the Carrer del Carme entrance stands the **Acàdemia de Medicina**, formerly the College of Surgery, and to the right, the wing for convalescents, now the **Institut d'Estudis Catalans**. Look for the frieze of 16th-century tiles on the life of St. Paul in its entryway. The hospital's courtyard is restful, with benches near orange trees that waft a sweet perfume in spring and are hung with golden fruit in summer. Exhibitions of art and

Learning to dance the sardana is part of growing up in Catalonia.

books are held in the various halls off the cloister. A gateway opens onto the Carrer de l'Hospital where the Fair of Sant Ponç on May 11 turns the street into a popular herb market.

Turn north from here up the Carrer del Angels, and you will reach the **Centre de Cultura Contemporania de Barcelona** on Carrer Montalegre. The Centre is a striking modern building and currently houses a small collection of contemporary art, including works by Tápies, Miró, and Chagall. The collection may be expanded on in the near future. Opening hours in winter are Tuesday, Thursday, and Friday 11:00 A.M. to 2:00 P.M. and 4:00 to 8:00 P.M. Wednesday and Saturday 11:00 A.M. to 8:00 P.M., Sunday 11:00 A.M. to 7:00 P.M. In summer the Centre is open Tuesday through Saturday 11:00 A.M. to 8:00 P.M., Sunday and holidays 11:00 A.M. to 7:00 P.M. Closed Mondays year round.

One more building on this side of the Ramblas that should not be missed is the small church of **Sant Pau del Camp**, off in a corner of its own at the end of the Carrer de Sant Pau, which starts at the Pla de la Boqueria. The simplicity of Sant Pau's Romanesque lines is an agreeable change from the extravagance of Barcelona's Modernisme and the intricacies of Gothic. The church was almost certainly built in the 800s, as the tomb of Wilfred II, dated 912, was found here. There is a lovely small cloister with curious, rather Arab-style arches. As the church is usually locked, the best time to see the interior is on a Sunday morning.

A few steps away is the broad Avinguda del Paral.lel, the funicular station for Montjuïc, or the short walk to the waterfront.

Waterfront

It is said that Barcelona turned its back on the sea in the 19th century and the city became more focused on its industries.

The sea wall where families loved to walk and catch the breeze on stifling summer nights was torn down. Access and even a view of the sea was obstructed by warehouses and railway tracks. Expansion was towards the hills, and La Barceloneta, created in the mid-1700s between the port and the beach, became the district of fishermen and sailors. Now all this has changed again, and a recreation area has been created along the waterfront.

Christopher Columbus, atop his 50-metre (164-feet) **Monument a Colom** at the foot of the Ramblas, has his back to the city, though Barcelona's boosters say he's pointing the way from his port to the Americas for the European Union. The cast-iron pillar was put up for the Universal Exposition of 1888. You can ride a lift (elevator) to a viewing platform in the globe beneath the statue and from there look down on the traffic whirling around the Plaça Portal de la Pau and the Passeig de Colom.

From the Columbus Statue take the wooden footbridge to cross over to the Moll d'Espanya. Considered to be an extension of the Ramblas it is referred to as the Rambla del Mar, and is popular with Sunday strollers. It leads to a shopping centre with 3-D cinema underneath its dome, and the **Aquarium de Barcelona**. One of Europe's largest aquariums, its main attraction is a spectacular glass tunnel on the sea bed. Opening hours are 10:00 A.M. to 9:00 or 10:00 P.M.

Nearby is a fleet of *golondrinas* (swallows) and *gaviotas* (gulls), excursion craft that tour the harbour, a pleasant way to spend a half hour. You'll pass under the aerial cable cars that link Montjuïc with La Barceloneta, and chug by the Royal Yacht Club and the docks of cruise ships and the ferries to Mallorca.

Just outside the port are floating platforms where mussels are grown on ropes underwater. Four grandiose buildings flank the plaza: the Port Authority *(Puerto Autónomo de Barcelona),* the naval headquarters *(Comandància de Marina),* the military headquarters *(Govern Militar),* and the customs house *(Aduana).* A skyscraper, the Torre Colom, is an unfortunate and more recent intrusion on the scene.

Revival of the old district around Sant Pau del Camp reveals vestiges of a more recent past.

Across from the Aduana is the only medieval shipyard still in existence, Les Reials Drassanes, begun in 1255. This is now the **Museu Marítim**, the Maritime Museum. The 16 bays of these yards could handle more than 30 galleys at a time and launched ships that extended Catalonia's dominion over the Mediterranean from Tunis to Greece, Sicily, Sardinia, and much of the French coast.

The museum presents models of ships, from the earliest galleys to the cargo and passenger vessels that have made Barcelona their home port up to the present day. The prize exhibit is the full-size copy of the Royal Galley, *La Reial*, aboard which Don Juan of Austria commanded the fleet that defeated the Turks at the Battle of Lepanto in 1571. Eighty Turkish galleys were sunk and 140 captured during the epic three-hour confrontation in which 30,000 Turks and 7,650 Christians died. The richly decorated red and gold galley, 60 metres (197 feet) long, was powered by 48 oars, each one pulled by three men.

The museum also has a fascinating collection of antique parchment maps, including one that belonged to Amerigo Vespucci. There are carved figureheads, naïvely painted sea chests, and primitive *ex voto* paintings made by sailors in thanks for surviving disasters at sea. A model of the wooden *Ictineo,* claimed to be the forerunner of the submarine, is displayed. Launched in 1859, it was designed to collect coral. Around the corner of the Drassanes is a stretch of the 14th-century third wall with towers.

A first step in upgrading the harbour area was converting the *Moll de Bosch i Alsina* (better known as the Moll de la Fusta, the wood-loading quay) into a broad promenade. Once again Barcelonans can stroll by the sea and take refreshment at the restaurants and bars. A large and convenient parking garage is located underneath.

Several impressive structures line the thoroughfare a little way inland called **Carrer Ample**, which roughly means "Broadway." Indeed, for a time the leaders of Barcelona society had their mansions in this street, as the large carriage entrances and ornamented patios of now-neglected buildings attest. Today, it and the parallel **Carrer de la Mercè** are favourites with students who crowd the smoky bars, stocked with wine barrels and with hams, sausages, and strings of garlic hanging from the ceilings.

Carrer Ample begins at the Plaça Duc de Medinaceli, a palm-lined square off the harbourside avenue, and passes the church of **La Mercè**, dedicated to the Mare del Déu de la Mercè, co-patroness of Barcelona with Santa Eulàlia. The Feast of La Mercè, in the last week of September when most of the tourists have gone, is one of the city's most popular celebrations.

The **convent of La Mercè**, now converted into the Capitania General, another military installation, was headquarters of an order created to ransom Catalans captured by Barbary Coast pirates. The great author of *Don Quixote*, Miguel de Cervantes, was such a prisoner and is supposed to have lived for a time at Number 2 Passeig de Colom, where he perhaps wrote the often-quoted praise of Barcelona, "Archive of courtesy, the stranger's refuge, shelter of the poor, home of the brave, avenger of the abused . . . unique for its site and beauty." The Carrer Ample and the Passeig de Colom end at the Central Post Office.

The most remarkable institution on this stretch of the waterfront is **La Llotja**—which has been a centre of Barcelona's trading activities for more than 600 years. It started out as an open loggia where merchants and ship owners made their deals. In the late 14th century this was enclosed and expanded to three naves of slim columns supporting high, round arches.

Here was installed the office of "Consulate of the Sea," the foundation of maritime law for all the Mediterranean countries. With the addition of a Neo-Classical façade, staircase, and upper storeys, the building served variously as a Chamber of Commerce and School of Fine Arts (where Picasso was a student) before becoming the **Barcelona Stock Exchange** *(Borsa de Barcelona)*. You can visit the exchange, from 9:00 A.M. to 5:00 P.M. After trading ends at noon, the place is still filled with hubbub and cigar smoke.

Under the arcades across the Passeig d'Isabell II is the stockbrokers' retreat, the Siete Puertas restaurant. Behind the arcades is a flourishing cut-price shopping area of watches, household appliances, and electronic wares. And here the harbour turns and La Barceloneta begins.

The only medieval shipyard still in existance, Barcelona's Les Drassanes (begun in 1255), is now the Museu Marítim.

La Barceloneta

La Barceloneta is not a "little Barcelona" as the name implies. It is separated from the city as much in spirit as by the physical barriers of water and the rail yards. No pompous banks, no hallowed Gothic shrines in this shirt-sleeve community of people who catch fish, cook and serve them, eat and drink heartily, and yell back and forth at each other across neighbourly streets.

La Barceloneta came into being to replace the Ribera district, demolished to make way for the Ciutadella fortress. A triangle of sand, the area now bordered by the Passeig Nacional, the Avinguda d'Icària, and the beachfront Passeig Marítim was chosen to house the dispossessed families. The triangle was divided into narrow blocks like boxcars, one apartment wide, so that every room could have windows for air and sun. Here, as in many quarters of Barcelona, the windows are shaded by *persianas*, long blinds that hang over the balcony edge to keep out the glare but let in the breeze. Fishermen unload their boats across the Passeig Nacional, and the catch soon finds its way to the scores of local bars and restaurants.

At the end of the harbour, turn in a block or two to the **Platja de Sant Miquel** (St. Michael's Beach). Once dominated by a row of flimsy wooden reataurants, the area was virtually rebuilt in preparation for the 1992 Olympics. It has since become one of the most fashionable out-of-town districts, with a cluster of elegant shops and several smart bars and restaurants. An extensive clean-up operation was carried out on the beaches, and a landscaped avenue established on the seafront leading to the Olympic port about a mile up the coast.

The Olympic Village itself is rapidly becoming absorbed into the rest of the community as the apartments which previously housed athletes are sold off to private residents. As the coast continues to the north a further mile of beaches has been landscaped and an attractive picnic zone has been created, a popular goal for day-trips from Barcelona. Some interesting industrial relics have been retained and renovated as a part of the scheme.

There is a good bus service to La Barceloneta—take the 17 or the 59 from the Plaça de Catalunya—and a sensational ride back can be had aboard a cabin of the 1,292-metre-long (4,238-foot-long) aerial **cable car** ride. Here the tower is 78 metres (256 feet) high, rising to 107 metres (351 feet) at the first stop above the harbour, where you can descend and walk back to the Columbus monument area, or continue on to Montjuïc at the level of the amusement park.

Montjuïc

Montjuïc, the playground of Barcelona, was the natural site for the 1992 Olympic Ring *(Anella Olímpica)* of athletic facilities. For many years its 210-metre (689-foot) summit has been a favourite excursion goal for its panoramic view of the city and harbour and for its outstanding complex of museums, amusement attractions, and sports facilities. In Roman times a road ran from the Mons Taber citadel to Mons Jovis, the mount of the god Jupiter for whom the hill is believed to be named. Others claim the origin is from Mons Judaicus or "Hill of the Jews," after a Jewish cemetery found on its slopes.

Traditionally, Montjuïc enjoyed two roles, that of a garden where olives and vines were cultivated and windmills turned in the breeze, and that of a lookout and fortress, where signal fires showed the way to ships at sea and where Spanish guns were pointed at the rebellious Catalan city rather than at any foreign invader. Montjuïc really came into its own as the site of the 1929 International Exhibition. The **Plaça d'Espanya**'s ornate fountain was created

Ride the cross-harbour cable car for thrills and a superb view.

to grace the entrance to the fairground. This is still a good point to begin a visit to Montjuïc, as it is a main metro and bus stop. The 1929 fair was a strange mixture of architectural styles. The gateway is marked by two brick columns reminiscent of St. Mark's Campanile in Venice. Then a number of hangar-type halls used during the year by commercial exhibitors at fairs line a central pedestrian avenue leading upwards to the vast **Palau Nacional**, the fair's Spanish pavilion.

This pompous, leaden pile, domed like the U.S. Capitol, has been redeemed to hold one of the world's finest collections of medieval art, the Museu Nacional d'Art de Catalunya (see pages 73–76). The one outstanding building of 1929 was the marble-and-glass German pavilion designed by Ludwig Mies Van der Rohe. It was taken down after the fair, a mistake rectified in the 1970s, when it was carefully reconstructed as the **Barcelona House**.

In the centre of the fairgrounds is the terrace of the **Font Màgica**, the truly "Magic Fountain." Saturday and Sunday, from 8:00 P.M. to midnight, the fountains perform a ballet of rising and falling jets bathed in a mist of changing colours set to music. Couples sit under the trees to listen or wander about with ice-cream cones while the flash bulbs of cameras wink like fireflies. Illuminated fountains rise on both sides of the central avenue down to the Plaça d'Espanya, and straight ahead above the city the lights of Tibidabo shine like an-swering beacon. Lit up at night, even the Palau Nacional seems a genuine palace.

Roads winding around the fairgrounds pass other attrac-tions. On the harbour side, off the Carrer de Lleida, is the **Mercat de les Flors**, a former flower market that is now a stage for avant-garde music, theatre, and dance. Tickets and information can be had at the Palau de la Virreina on the Ramblas. Up the hill and across the street is the **Museu Arqueològic** (Archaeological Museum). Among the many interesting exhibits drawn mainly from prehistoric, Iberian, Greek, and Roman sites in Catalonia are reconstructions of tombs and life-like dioramas. Just beyond on the other side of the road is the outdoor **Teatre Grec** (Greek Theatre), built in 1929. In summer, when Barcelona's regular the-atres would be uncomfortably warm, the action moves here. Around another curve within walking distance up the hill is the **Museu Etnològic** (Ethnological Museum). This modern and well-presented collection usually has a special programme highlighting the native arts of Latin America and other lands. The Palau de la Virreina will tell you what is currently on display here and give you the programme of the Greek Theatre.

A giant lobster and sea breezes draw crowds to harbour cafés.

Farther up Montjuïc and left where the Avinguda de l'Estadi, the Olympic Ring boulevard, becomes the Avinguda de Miramar is the simple and elegant **Fundació Joan Miró**. The museum was designed in 1975 by the architect Josep Lluís Sert to receive the paintings, drawings, tapestries, and sculpture donated by Miró himself and by contemporary artists and collectors. Sert, a Barcelonan and friend of Miró, was dean of the School of Architecture at Harvard University. Miró died in 1983 at the age of 90.

The exhibits follow Miró's artistic development from 1914 onwards. Photographs show him always neatly dressed and barbered, looking like a Catalan businessman in contrast to the Bohemian Picasso, and in contrast, too, with the far-out abstraction he created. The entire collection is witty and bright with the reds, yellows, blues, and black always associated with the artist. Note the large *Tapís de la Fundació* tapestry (1979), burly, ropy, and powerfully coloured. The *Woman Dreaming of Evasion* (1945), *Morning Star* (1946), and *Claro de Luna* (1968) here are among his finest works. Sert's white concrete building was awarded a special prize in 1977 by the Council of Europe. It is beautifully and naturally lit by the sun through unseen skylights. A pleasant garden restaurant in the museum serves a light lunch and refreshments.

The Avinguda de Miramar continues past the station of the funicular railway that climbs the hill from the Avinguda del Paral.lel near the Paral.lel metro stop. The funicular links up here with a cable car that goes to the **Parc d'Atraccions de Montjuïc**, an amusement park, and on to the **Castell de Montjuïc** on the summit. Cars run daily in summer, weekends only in winter. A short walk from the amusement park is the Plaça de l'Armada station for the cable car that crosses the harbour, completing an interesting network of transport by cable.

The fortress atop Montjuïc, built in 1640, remained in use by the army and then as a prison until shortly before it was turned over to the city for a museum in 1960. The

The Palau Nacional's domes loom majestically on Montjuïc's flank.

Museu Militar (Military Museum) has an extensive collection of antique weaponry and armour, lead soldiers of different epochs, and models of Catalan castles. Here in a basement room you'll find what may be the only statue of Generalíssimo Francisco Franco to be seen in Barcelona today. The fort has sombre associations for the city. Its cannons bombarded the population to put down rebellions in the 18th and 19th centuries, and it was the site of political executions, including that of Lluís Companys, president of the Generalitat of Catalonia during the Civil War, who was shot by a firing squad in 1940.

The far slope of Montjuïc below the fortress is occupied by the **Cementiri del Sud-Ouest**. From the airport road, the tombs look like windows in the mountainside. Many patriots are buried here, some in a common grave, the Fossar de la Pedrera. The present generation has healed the bitter divisions of that cruel war and the dictatorship that followed. It is a subject today's Spain has consigned to history.

The Olympic facilities, on the northern side of Montjuïc, are centred on the stadium and Plaça d'Europa. The most handsome building is the **Palau d'Esports Sant Jordi**, designed by Japanese architect Arata Izozaki. It can seat 17,000 under a roof 45 metres (148 feet) high.

The **Poble Espanyol** (Spanish Village), on Montjuïc's northeastern flank, is an attraction for which the cliché "fun for the whole family" might have been invented. It's a composite of Spain's varied regions, each represented by replicas of real houses, church towers, fountains, plazas, and palaces built of solid brick and stone. The entrance, through one of the gates of the walled city of Avila, is the first step into a community of 115 such reproductions arranged along a network of 18 streets and alleys and 11 village squares.

In the Poble Espanyol you can go to the theatre (or children's theatre), listen to a band concert or live jazz, see a street festival, do your Christmas shopping (and go to a bank), have an elaborate meal or just a snack of tapas in a bar, dance in a discotheque or to an orchestra, see a film, or watch a flamenco performance. In a park of more than 4.6 hectares (11.4 acres) there are 13 restaurants, 6 bars, 34 workshops where artisans make regional handicrafts, and scores of shops offering these and other typically Spanish products. The **Museu d'Industrias i Art Popular** (Museum of Traditional Arts and Crafts), where some of these things are being made, is installed in a series of buildings.

One of the most impressive reconstructions is the bell tower, in brick and tile, of the Aragonese church of Utebo; behind it is the Andalusian quarter, all whitewashed alleys, geraniums, forged-iron grills, and lanterns.

Magic Fountain's jets dance in a ballet of sound and colour.

A 20-minute multi-media show entitled "**The Barcelona Experience**" uses 44 projectors and some 2,500 slides and film clips to cover the city's history and high spots. Cannons boom and heads roll. There's a touching scene of Pau (Pablo) Casals in his nineties speaking at the United Nations and saying "Catalunya was the greatest country in the world."

The Poble Espanyol is fun to visit at night as well as by day. It opens at 10:00 A.M. The museum and shops close at 3:00 P.M., but the action in restaurants, cabarets, and discotheques goes on until 2:00 A.M. (6:00 A.M. Thursdays to Saturdays). A

Woman meets "Woman" at the Fundació Joan Miró.

free double-decker London bus shuttles between the Poble Espanyol and the Plaça d'Espanya until the metro closes at 11:00 P.M. The attraction was built for the 1929 fair.

The **Museu Nacional d'Art de Catalunya** in the Palau Nacional at the top of the fairgrounds is unmatched in the world for Romanesque art and for Gothic painting of the Catalan school. It has undergone extensive refurbishment over recent years, and the section on Romanesque art is now finally reopened. Check before you visit if you are interested in the other collections (tel. 423 71 99).

From the ninth to the 13th centuries more than 2,000 churches were built in Catalonia in the Romanesque style of thick, bare walls with rounded arches for doors, windows, and cloisters. Interiors were decorated by frescoes in the Byzantine tradition, by primitive sculpture of biblical episodes or rural life on the capitals of columns, by painted altar front panels, and by carved wooden crosses and Madonnas of great purity. Around the turn of this century many of these works of art were removed to Catalan museums from churches that were deteriorating or abandoned, thus saving them from further damage or being sold out of the country.

Some of the very best are in this museum, such as the great 12th-century *Christ Pantocrator* from the apse of the church of Sant Climent de Taüll in the Pyrenees. Look for the ingenuous painting of the martyrdom of Saints Quirze and Julita, getting sawed in half, heads stuck with nails, and finally, while being boiled in oil, still able to look with calm disdain on their frustrated torturers. A superb group of unpainted, elongated wooden figures representing the descent from the cross is from the church of Santa Maria de Taüll. There are masterpieces in every room of this most unusual collection.

The Gothic wing is excellent, too. The first section is arranged to place the scenes, people, and symbols of the art in the social and historical context of the feudal period. A lot of the paintings are *retablos*, many-panelled screens with Gothic-arched frames that stood behind chapel altars. Often the backgrounds show homely furnishings and unaffected glimpses of everyday life. Mostly from the 14th to 16th centuries, the paintings begin to show the influence of Spain's Flemish and Italian possessions, though they are almost exclusively religious art.

Among the prizes in this wing are Lluís Dalmau's *Virgin of the Councillors*, with its portraits, full of character, of the

N

CARRER DE PI I MARGALL
T. DE GRACIA
CARRER DE GRACIA
T. DE GRACIA
T. DE GRACIA
CARRER DE GRACIA
CARRER DE SANT ANTONI MARIA CLARET
CARRER DE INDUSTRIA
PASSEIG DE SANT JOAN
CARRER DE BAILEN
CARRER DE
AVINGUDA DIAGONAL
CARRER DE CORSEGA
CARRER DE ROSSELLO
CARRER DE PROVENÇA
CARRER DE MALLORCA
CARRER DE VALÈNCIA
CARRER D'ARAGO
AV. DE GAUDI
CARRER DEL DOS DE MAIG
CARRER DE DOS DE MAIG
CARRER DE CARTEGENA
CARRER DE CASTILLEJOS
CARRER DE PADILLA
LA MERIDIANA
GRAN VIA DE LES CORTS CATALANES
Plaça de les
Glories Catalanes
Plaça de Toros
Monumental
AVINGUDA DE
PASSEIG DE CARLES I
ALMOGAVERS
C. DE PALLARS
C. DE LLULL
CARRER DE WELLINGTON
CARRER DE SARDENYA
CARRER DE SICILIA
CARRER DE NAPOLS
CARRER DE MARC
BRUC
CARRER DE PAU CLARIS
C. DE CONSELL DE CENT
RAMBLA DE CATALUNYA
PASSEIG DE GRACIA
CARRER DE BALMES
CARRER DE LA DISPUTACIO
C. DE CASP
C. DE D'AUSIAS MARC
CARRERS
DELS
PASSEIG DE
PUJADES
P. DE PICASSO
Parc de la
Ciutadella
R. DE SANT PERE
VIA LAIETANA
LA RAMBLA
Plaça de la
Catalunya
Plaça de la
Universitat
Mercat
del Born
Estació
Termini
GRAN VIA DE LES CORTS CATALANES
R. DE SANT ANTONIO
C. COMTE D'URGELL
CARRER COMTE BORRELL
C. DE VILAMAR
C. DE ARAGO
CARRER DE

Barcelona

Teatre del
Liceu
CARRER NOU DE LA RAMBLA
PG. DE COLOM
Plaça Portal
de la Pau
Museo
Maritim
AV. DEL PARAL·LEL
CINTURO DEL LITORAL
Moll d'Espanya
PASSEIG NACIONAL
PASSEIG MARITIM
Mediterranean

| 0 | .25 | .5 mi |
| 0 | .25 | .5 km |

politicos who commissioned the work for the City Hall chapel in 1445; Jaume Ferrer II's stylishly hatted *St. Jerome*; a curious, very original set of four wooden tomb panels of mourners in striped tubular gowns fleeing, as if from some terrible catastrophe; a very fine retable of St. John the Baptist with Saints Sebastian and Nicholas. And just before the exit, look for Ayne Bru's gory throat-slitting of San Cugat in which the saint's dog is snoozing through the whole nasty business. The ceramics section on an upper floor has examples of Arab sculpture and tiles.

The museum is presently undergoing renovation. Check with museum officials for open hours, tel. 423 18 24.

La Ciutadella

On the opposite side of Barcelona from Montjuïc, above the harbour, the cannons of another fort (now converted to a park) once bracketed the city: the infamous Ciutadella, or Citadel. It's a lovely park, too, with a lake, large old trees, and pleasant pathways successfully erasing the memory of a grim episode.

When Barcelona surrendered to the troops of King Philip V after a 13-month siege in 1714 (see page 17), a large fort was constructed on this site to keep the city in line. To make room for La Ciutadella, the fishermen's community of La Ribera was obliterated, including 1,262 houses that were torn down without compensation. To add insult to injury, Barcelona had to pay the costs of building the hated fortress. Although La Ciutadella never saw any military action, it was used as a prison and place of execution, and the place became a symbol of oppression, like the Bastille. "Down with La Ciutadella!" was the cry during demonstrations, and great was the joy when it was finally demolished in 1869. All that's left of the original fort are the chapel, governor's palace (now a school), and the arsenal, today divided between the Museu d'Art Modern and the seat of the Parlament de Catalunya. The past was exorcized in 1888 when, redesigned as a park, it became the site of the Universal Exposition that celebrated Barcelona's emergence as a modern metropolis.

The **Arc del Triomf** in Moorish-style brickwork was designed by Josep Vilaseca, and erected as the entrance to the fair at the end of what is now the Plaça Lluís Companys, across the Passeig de Pujades from the park. A statue of Rafael Casanova once stood in this plaza and served as the rallying point for nationalist demonstrations every September 11. The imposing red-brick **Castell dels Tres Dragons,** Gothic inspired, was designed by Modernist architect Domènech as a café and restaurant for the 1888 Exhibition, and now houses the Museu de Zoologia. Although lacking the elegance of many of the city's Modernist buildings, it is a particularly good example of Domènech's rationalistic style.

The main attraction of the **Museu d'Art Modern** is its collection of 19th- and early 20th-century Catalan works, particularly those of the Modernist school. It is intended that the art collection will be moved to the Museu d'Art de Catalunya on Montjuïc so that the entire building can be used by the regional parliament.

There are some notable canvases by Santiago Rusiñol and Ramon Casas, including the amusing painting of the latter on a tandem bicycle with Pere Romeu which hung in the Els Quatre Gats café. This artists' hangout on the Carrer Montsió was where Picasso had his first show in 1900. There is a collection of Casas charcoal portraits with one of the young Picasso (1901), and a stone bust of the painter looking like a roughneck, with a cockeyed grin and hair over one eye (1931) by Pau Gargallo. Other works include those of Modernist artists Mir and Nonell.

Romanesque frescoes are among the gems of the Catalan art museum's collection.

The plastic arts are well represented here with collections of Modernist furniture, including designs by Gaudí, and Gaspar Homar, ceramics by Antoni Serra and jewellery by the Masriera family. Finally, don't miss the avant-garde sculptures by Gonzalez and Gargallo. Opening hours are 10:00 A.M. to 7:00 P.M. Tuesday to Sunday; guided tours are available to groups only and are at noon and 5:00 P.M.

About a third of the park is the **Barcelona Zoo** *(Parc Zoològic)*. It is well laid out under trees, and many enclosures are behind moats, without bars. A star performer is Copito de Nieve (Snowflake), a rare albino gorilla who will sometimes come to the edge of his moat when called by name. There is a show of performing dolphins a number of times daily. Near the marine theatre is a beloved Barcelona **fountain**, the lady with an umbrella whose spokes drip water onto her out-

stretched hand. The zoo opens daily from 9:30 A.M. to 7:30
P.M. in summer, and 10:00 A.M. to 5:00 P.M. in winter.

The Diagonal

The broad, tree-lined Avinguda Diagonal slices across
Cerdà's grid of blocks from the coast to the hills. He designed it for through traffic and it links up with the ring roads
around the city and the toll highways beyond. It's largely industrial around the **Plaça de les Glòries Catalanes**, a busy
roundabout linking main roads into the city, but becomes
more dignified to the west after crossing the Passeig de Sant
Joan. Between the Passeig de Gràcia and the Plaça de
Francesc Macià it is positively elegant, with four-star hotels
and luxury shops. Pricey restaurants and discotheques
abound in adjoining streets. The districts on the hillside beyond were once separate villages, which have been gradually
absorbed over the years by Barcelona's expansion. Each still
preserves its own unique character.

Gràcia, for example, has its own town square, the Plaça
Rius i Taulet, and streets named Llibertat and Fraternitat and
a Plaça Revolució that reflect its radical past. There's a great
night-time blowout of food and festivity in these streets in
the second half of August. Beyond Gràcia, at the end of the
Avenida de Gaudí, is the astonishing **Hospital de Sant Pau**,
designed by Domènech and completed by his son.

Horta, near the site of the Olympic velodrome, is farther
out. On its fringes, set in the park of an aristocratic estate, is
the amusing Laberint, a 200-year-old maze of yew hedge usually filled with squealing kids and flustered teachers. The atmosphere of **Sarrià** and **Pedralbes** is patrician—villas with
gardens and the city's most expensive real estate. The **Monestir de Pedralbes** has a superb Gothic church and a charming
two-storeyed cloister. Queen Elisenda de Montcada, who

founded the convent in 1326, is buried here. Two rooms have been converted into an art gallery housing part of the Thyssen-Bornemisza collection, including important works from the medieval to Italian Baroque periods. The monastery and art collection are open from 10:00 A.M. to 2:00 P.M., except Mondays, and until 5:00 P.M. on Saturdays. Pedralbes can be reached on the regional railway from the Plaça de Catalunya.

After the Plaça de Francesc Macià on the Diagonal are the most modern office buildings, faculties of the university, and the latest hotels, with a huge shopping centre, l'Illa, housing all the major chain shops as well as restaurants and a supermarket. The 120,000-seat stadium of the Barcelona football club is between the Diagonal and Montjuïc here.

On the other side of the avenue, surrounded by a park, is the **Palau Reial de Pedralbes**, an estate of the Güell family converted into a royal residence in 1924 in case King Alfonso XIII should drop by. It now houses elements of the **Museu de les Artes Decoratives** and a collection of carriages. Renaissance- and Baroque-period paintings from the **Colecció Cambó**, formerly in the Palau de la Virreina, are now hung here. Be sure to go around the park walls to see the dragon gate in wrought iron designed by Gaudí for the Güells.

La Sagrada Família

What the Eiffel Tower is to Paris or the Statue of Liberty is to New York, the spires of the Sagrada Família church are to Barcelona. They are the immediately recognizable symbol of the city, their spiky profile visible from afar, and unmistakable, for there is nothing remotely like them in the world. Few people who have not seen the eight peculiar, cigar-shaped perforated towers realize that they only mark the shell of a church that was begun in 1882 and is still far from completion. Fewer still are aware that if Antoni Gaudí's plans are followed, ten more towers will be added surrounding a 170-metre (558-feet) central spire as tall as the Washington Monument.

Gaudí died in 1926 at the age of 74 and was buried in the crypt. During his last years he lived in a room inside the construction site, obsessed with the project. A museum in the crypt has models and drawings that show what the finished building would look like, but Gaudí did not leave detailed plans. During his lifetime he completed the crypt begun by an earlier architect and supervised work on the east Portal of the Nativity, one tower, and part of the apse and nave.

The west Portal of the Passion and its towers have been under construction by other architects following his style since 1952. The main Portal of the Resurrection on the Carrer de Mallorca has not been started.

The east façade shows best what Gaudí intended. Everything has significance and a name, and no space is left unfilled. The three doorways, with stonework dripping like stalactites, represent Faith, Hope, and Charity, and are loaded with sculpture depicting the birth and youth of Jesus, angel choirs and musicians, the Flight into Egypt, the Slaughter of the Innocents, the Tree of Calvary, and much, much more. Seeds and wild-flowers found on the site surmount some of

Copito de Nieve (Snowflake) is the star inhabitant of the Barcelona Zoo.

the towers and others are upheld at the base by tortoises, or entwined in vines, crawled over by snails and embellished with all kinds of other living things. The cathedral is intended to incorporate every aspect of creation and faith. Twelve towers, four at each portal, are to represent the Apostles; four higher ones, the Evangelists; a dome over the apse, the Virgin; and the central spire, the Saviour. An elevator and steps give access to a look-out from one of the east towers. On the west side, large letters in orange tile

Highlights of Modernist Barcelona

Antoni Gaudí

Casa Battló (1904) Passeig de Gràcia 43 (see page 52)

Casa Milà "La Pedrera" (1905-1910) Passeig de Gracia 92 (see pages 52–53)

Palau Güell (1904) Carrer Nou de la Rambla (see page 51)

Sagrada Família (1882-present) (see pages 80–83)

Parc Güell (1900-1914) (see pages 83–84)

Lluís Domènech i Montaner

Casa Lleó Morera (1905) Passeig de Gràcia 35 (see page 51)

Castell dels Tres Dragons (1888) Parc de la Ciutadella (see page 77)

Hospital de Sant Pau (1902–1930) Avinguda de Gaudí

Palau de la Música Catalana (1898) Carrer de Sant Pere més Alt (see pages 54–56)

Josep Puig i Cadafalch

Casa Amatller (1898) Passeig de Gràcia 41 (see page 52)

Casa Macaya (1901) Puig de Sant Joan 108

Casa de les Punxes (1903-1905) Avenida Diagonal 416-420 (see page 50)

proclaim "Sanctus," and "Hosanna in Excelsis" is executed in "broken-plate" mosaic.

With all this exuberance, the basic design is still recognizably rooted in Barcelona's Gothic tradition. In the Sagrada Família, Gaudí went beyond the Art Nouveau of his Modernist peers to create something new and highly personal. Whether or not it will ever be finished is a matter of controversy. Funds from private contributions trickle in at a pace that barely keeps the work ticking over. Some critics say the best thing to do now would be to take down the cranes and hoardings, plant grass amid the typically Gaudian tilted columns of the nave, and turn it into a park.

Tibidabo

The first bright, clear morning of your visit, head for Tibidabo, the 542-metre (1,778-foot) peak that overlooks Barcelona. Families come here on summer evenings to enjoy the amusement park, but you can also visit the museum of working automatons, climb the 50-metre (164-foot) watch tower, or visit the church of the Sagrat Corazon. A neo-Gothic work by Enric Sagnier, the church is surmounted by a monumental figure of Christ which is one of the city's landmarks.

To reach the summit take the train (not metro) to "Av. Tibidabo" from the Plaça de Catalunya. From here a blue tram runs daily in the summer, Saturdays and Sundays the rest of the year, taking you up to the funicular station. Five minutes on the funicular lifts you through pine woods to the top, where you have a spectacular panorama of the city, the sea coast, and, on very clear days, both Mallorca and the Pyrenees.

Parks

On the rising slope of the hills behind Gràcia, the **Parc Güell** is a compendium of Gaudí's most distinctive devices in a setting of shady paths that overlook the city and the sea. Count Güell bought 6 hectares (15 acres) here, intending to create a community of villas, and in 1900 gave Gaudí carte blanche to produce something original. For the next 14 years, on and off, the architect evidently had fun with the assignment. From the entrance on the Carrer d'Olot, where his gingerbread gatehouse stands beside a forged-iron portal, to the tilted tunnel walkways, dripping with cave-like encrustations, atop the hill, Gaudí's trademarks are omnipresent.

There's the familiar double cross on spires, a dragon, slanted columns, an egg, acres of broken ceramic surfaces (glazed to Gaudí's order and smashed for him), mask-eyes as windows, and a Gaudian patchwork of colours and contours. Here is the famous serpentine wall of tile mosaic that serves also as a winding bench around a raised plaza.

This space, which regularly inspires impromptu *sardana* dancing, is supported beneath by the **Saló de les Cent Columnes** (Hall of the One Hundred Columns). There actually are 86, Doric in style, in what was to have been the colony's covered market. If you look closely at the ceiling, you'll see dolls' heads, bottles, glasses, and plates stuck in the mosaics.

As a real-estate venture the park failed to attract buyers. Only two villas were built. Gaudí lived for a time in one, with a gold-flecked witch's-hat tower. It contains a small museum of furniture by Gaudí and other memorabilia. The property became a park in 1923. It is open from 10:00 A.M. to 2:00 P.M. and 4:00 to 7:00 P.M. from June through September. The 24 bus from the Plaça de Catalunya goes to the park.

The city has created a number of interesting parks for the benefit of otherwise neglected neighbourhoods. The **Parc de l'Espanya Industrial**, for example, converted a factory adjoining the Sants railway station into a lake and waterfalls

The awe-inspiring spires of Gaudí's Sagrada Família are synonymous with Barcelona.

with contemporary sculpture. Miró's giant abstract figure *Woman and Bird* in the **Parc Joan Miró** near the Plaça d'Espanya can be seen from afar.

The **Parc de la Creueta del Coll** has won the praise of art critics for works by Ellsworth Kelly, Roy Liechtenstein, and Eduardo Chillida. The park was built on the side of an abandoned quarry in the working-class Carmelo district. Chillida's striking red concrete claw hangs by cables over a man-made lake.

Excursions

 Montserrat

The sandstone reef of Montserrat rises out of the Llobregat plain 62 kilometres (38 miles) northwest of Barcelona in the very heart of Catalonia. Although the view from its 1,235-metre (4,051-foot) summit can encompass both the Pyrenees and Mallorca, it is more significant that from afar one can see the unmistakable serrated outline that gives Montserrat its name, the "Saw Mountain." Montserrat is not on the road to anywhere, yet all roads in Catalonia symbolically lead to Montserrat, the shrine of Catalan nationhood. The landscape is much like the rocky ridges in cowboy movies where the hero and villain shoot it out between the boulders.

The first hermitages on the mountain were perhaps established to escape the Moorish invasion. One such hermitage, dedicated to St. Mary, was enlarged as a Benedictine monastery in the 11th century. Some one hundred years later it became the repository of **La Moreneta**, the Little Dark Madonna, a small wooden image of a brown-faced Virgin holding the infant Jesus on her lap and the globe in her right hand. Pilgrims, from commoners to kings, have climbed the mountain to worship her ever since. She has a special importance to Catalans as their patron, and, like Catalan nationalism, the monastery has been destroyed only to rise again. It was burned to the ground by Napoleon's soldiers in 1808, abandoned in 1835 when all convents were sequestered by the state, and rebuilt only in 1874. During the Spanish Civil War, when anti-clerical feelings were violent among the Republicans in Barcelona, La Moreneta was secretly replaced by a copy, and the original was hidden during the Franco years. When Catalan language and traditions were suppressed, Montserrat's monks continued to say masses in Catalan and kept the flame alive.

Saw-tooth ridge of Montser-rat shelters its world-famed monastery, the shrine of Catalan nationhood.

The site is spectacular, tucked in folds of rock high above the plain. A million pilgrims and tourists visit the monastery each year. On the eve of the saint's day, April 27, the monks hold an all-night vigil attended by crowds of people. But almost any day of the week scores of busloads of Catalans disgorge in front of the complex of museum, souvenir supermarket, and cafeteria. Many are on village outings, carrying banners and accompanied by a *cobla* of musicians to play as they dance the *sardana* in the large square before the church. A *cobla* will have reedy oboes and horns, and a drummer playing a flageolet while beating a drum tied to his arm. Sometimes half a dozen *sardana* circles bob up and down at once, filling the square.

A long queue forms to see La Moreneta in the basilica. She looks down from a gold-and-glass case above and to the right of the altar, but the faithful can touch or kiss her right hand through an opening. She looks much like other Madonnas in Barcelona's Museu d'Art de Catalunya. At 1:00 and 7:10 P.M. (except in July), the choir boys of the

Escolania, one of the world's oldest music schools, founded in the 13th century, fill the basilica with their angelic voices. The massed congregation joins in at the end of the service to sing Montserrat's hymn, the *Virolai*, an expression of faith fused with a nationalist fervour.

The spires of rock above the monastery are a favourite goal of climbers. While watching them, you can have a snack in the open-air market where local honey and a soft goat yoghurt are served in little cups. The monks distill a sweet liqueur called *Aromas de Montserrat* using herbs

Sitges, with its beautiful beaches, is a popular spot for both Barcelonans and tourists.

found on the mountain. From the monastery there are walks to other hermitages and a funicular to the cave sacred to the legend of the Madonna. Statues and plaques line the paths.

Montserrat can be reached easily from Barcelona by train from the Plaça d'Espanya. On arrival at L'Aire de Montserrat station, a cable car takes you right up to the monastery. A bus service also operates from Barcelona by Autocares Julià (tel. 490 40 00). By car, leave Barcelona via the Diagonal and go onto the highway, direction Tarragona, exiting at Sortida 25.

Sitges

It's easy to get to the Costa Dorada beaches from Barcelona. The coast south of the city earned its name from its broad, golden sands, in contrast to the rocky coves of the Costa Brava to the north. The goal of a day's outing should be Sitges, the favourite resort of the Barcelonans themselves. The 43-km (27-mile) drive is uninspiring until you get to **Castelldefels**. This is still less than half an hour by train from the city. There's a substantial castle a bit inland, more impressive from a distance than close up.

The coast drive is a scenic but narrow and curvy route that after another half-hour brings **Sitges** into view. If you prefer you can by-pass this drive by taking the toll road, which gets you to Sitges in 8 minutes. Happily, the town has escaped the high-rises and tawdry atmosphere of many coastal resorts, although it does get somewhat overwhelmed by crowds in summer. There are two beaches, separated by a promontory where gleaming whitewashed houses cluster around the church of Sant Bartomeu. The **Museu d'El Cau Ferrat** is installed in the house of the painter Santiago Rusinol (1861–1931), whose collection of works by El Greco, Ramon Casas, Picasso, and others is on display, along with many of his own works. Across the street, the **Museu Mar i Cel** (Sea and Sky Museum) holds a small collection of medieval sculpture and paintings in a splendid house overlooking the sea.

La Ribera, the nearest beach, is almost 3 kilometres (2 mile) long, backed by a promenade lined with cafés and restaurants. The streets are carpeted with flowers for the procession of Corpus Christi in late spring.

On the hillsides and lanes are the villas of wealthy Barcelona families, while the streets between the beach and railway station are geared to food and frolic.There's one more curiosity, the **Museu Romantica**'s large family of antique dolls.

WHAT TO DO

SPORTS

Barcelona's successful bid for the 1992 Olympic Games was its third try this century. To support the succession of Olympic candidacies, it developed a superb network of playing fields, tracks, courts, pools, and riding rings. The visitor won't have any difficulty keeping in shape here, whether by joining the joggers in the parks of Montjuïc, swimming at a beach, playing tennis, or enjoying almost any sport. Even skiing in the Pyrenees is only a few hours away.

At the Reial Club de Golf El Prat near the airport, 27 holes provide three different circuits. Clubs and carts may be rented and there's also a pool. The Club de Golf Vallromanes is only 23 km (14 miles) from the city, and the Terramar course near Sitges is about an hour's drive away. Other nearby courses are at Sant Cugat, off the A-7 motorway, and the nine-hole course at Sant Andreu de Llavaneres on the A-19 towards Mataró.

Tennis courts open to the public are located in Pedralbes in the Can Caralleu sports centre, where there are also indoor and outdoor swimming pools. The courts are open from 8:00 A.M. to 11:00 P.M. For information phone 203 78 74. Your hotel may also be able to arrange guest privileges at a Barcelona tennis club. Squash courts are available at Squash Barcelona, Av. Dr. del Marañón 17, tel. 334 02 58.

For sailing information, you can contact the Reial Club Marítim, tel. 315 00 07.

Skiing may be the fastest-growing sport in Catalonia. Each year brings new developments in the Pyrenees, most within a few hours of Barcelona: Núria, at 1,963 metres (6,439 feet); La Molina, whose slopes rise to 2,537 metres (8,321 feet); and

Vallter, with 12 slopes and a top station at 2,500 metres (8,200 feet). Information on the conditions of roads and slopes can be obtained from the Associació Catalana d'Estacions d'Esquí, tel. (93) 416 09 09.

The great spectator sport in Barcelona is football, and football means the Barça. The top-ranked team of the F.C. Barcelona has a 120,000-seat stadium, Camp Nou. Consult a newspaper for dates and times of games.

Treasures of this historically rich city can be found in many antiques shops.

La Corrida de Toros, the bullfight, has never held the place in Catalonia that it enjoys in the south of Spain. The Plaza de Toros Monumental on the Gran Vía at Passeig de Carles I, usually has something going on Sunday afternoons at 5:30 P.M. from spring through autumn.

SHOPPING

In Barcelona you'll find handicrafts from every corner of the country. As a city of style and taste, Barcelona also abounds in fashion boutiques, antiques shops, and art galleries. Just remember that, with the exception of the big department stores, most shops are closed between 1:30 and 4:30 P.M. and stay open until as late as 8:00 P.M. or after.

Behind the cathedral is the place to go for ceramics, both the traditional tiles, plates, pitchers, and bowls in white glaze with blue and yellow decoration, and modern creations. You can browse for hours in the antiques shops in narrow streets of the Barri Gòtic, such as the Carrer dels Banys Nous. Many of the offerings are frankly copies, but good copies and sold as such. You'll find copper vessels, chests, old tiles, swords, old medical instruments, clocks, furniture. More of this on a knicknack level is spread out on the stands of dealers at the fair held on Thursdays in the Plaça Nova.

The Passeig de Gràcia, the fashionable streets leading off it in the direction of the Rambla de Catalunya, and also the Diagonal in this area are good hunting grounds for men's and women's fashions. Leather jackets and skirts are good value. The latest vogue is to bring together a dozen or so arcades or a gallery that burrows into a block and winds around inside in a blaze of light and music, like El Boulevard Rosa and the Galerías Halley on the Passeig de Gràcia. El Boulevard dels Antiquaris at 57 Passeig de Gràcia does the same thing for antiques, with 73 shops under one roof.

> **A chemist's is called farmacia (fahrmahthyah), and they don't sell books, film, newspapers, toilet articles, or cosmetics.**

Down the Ramblas you'll find good bookstores and a variety of shops that sell such souvenirs as bullfight posters with your name on them and the leather (or plastic) wineskin called a *bota*, and its glass relative, the *porrón*; imitation Toledo steel with the engraving painted on; imitation duelling pistols; and authentically tawdry sex-shop trinkets. There are leather factories off the Rambla de Santa Mónica on the Carrer Ample.

A selection of better-quality handicrafts and curios can be found in the Poble Espanyol on Montjuïc. If your thing is stamps and coins, go to the Plaça Reial on Sunday morning, or to the Sant Antoni market, which also sells records and books.

Barcelona's flea market, Els Encants, stretches northwards from the Plaça de les Glòries Catalanes and is open

Pastry shop's Art Nouveau decor is a delightful confection too.

Monday, Wednesday, Friday, and Saturday. On the same plaza is a huge new shopping mall, if the secondhand wares do not appeal. Non-E.U. residents can reclaim I.V.A. tax (Value Added Tax, anything from 6 to 33 percent depending on the type of goods), and if purchases are substantial it is certainly worthwhile to fill out the forms in the shop. The refund will be mailed to your home address after your return. You must show your purchases to the customs inspector on departure and give him the appropriate forms.

One-stop shopping can be done in the big department store El Corte Inglés on Plaza Catalunya, at 617 or 471 Avenida Diagonal, or at 19 Avenida Portal del Angel.

NIGHTLIFE

Even when the sun goes down, Barcelona shines. It's a swinging city with every kind of nightlife diversion. In good weather, which is most of the time, the streets at night are slow-moving rivers of strollers. The main churches and monuments are illuminated, taking on a new and graceful aspect. The interior light shining through the stained-glass windows

FESTIVALS

January 5/6 *Día de Reyes* (Three Kings Day), gift giving and pyrotechnical displays.

February Feast of Santa Eulàlia, parades of *gigantes*, medieval dances.

March/April Carnival at beginning of Lenten season. Holy Week *(Semana Santa)* with series of religious festivals starting with Palm Sunday procession through Rambla de Catalunya.

April 23 Feast of Sant Jordi, impromptu book stalls are set up and couples exchange flowers.

April 27 Feast of Virgin of Montserrat, liturgical acts, choir singing, and *sardana* dancing.

May 11 Feast of Sant Ponç, herb fair in Carrer de l'Hospital.

June Corpus Christi, carpets of flowers and processions in Sitges, also the curious tradition of a "dancing egg" balanced on the spray of the cathedral fountain.

June 23–24 Feast of Sant Joan, big blowout with fireworks and feasting.

End June–July *Grec* festival of theatre, classical, pop, and rock music.

August 15 Local block parties in the festooned streets of Gràcia in week leading up to Assumption.

September 11 *Diada*, Catalan national day, demonstrations and flag waving.

September 24 A week of celebrations in honour of the city's patron, Mare del Déu de la Mercè (Our Lady of Mercy). The Ramblas become an outdoor banquet hall, the squares bandstands, and the streets dance floors.

December 6–24 Fairs for Christmas crib figurines—the most important is for in front of the cathedral.

of the cathedral and the lamplight of narrow lanes in the Barri Gòtic bring out details that you miss by day.

The city authorities subsidize concerts, from rock to classical, in the Plaça de Catalunya and in neighbourhood parks. The world's great singers appear in opera at the Gran Teatre del Liceu (though not since the fire there in 1994), while the latest in modern dance, music, and experimental theatre is regularly staged in the evenings at the Mercat de les Flors, the old flower market a short walk from the spectacular sound-and-light show of the Font Màgica (see page 68).

The young crowd flock to "design bars" for an after-work drink or an evening of disco dancing. A design bar is an ultra-modern environment. For example, entering Nick Havana (Carrer Rosselló 208), one of the pioneers of the design bar genre, is like emerging into a small square. The bar is divided in various sections, each surrounded by café-style tables to form different centres for groups. The disco area with multi-vision images flashing on one wall is separated by a glass panel from a sound-proofed conversation area for those who want to sit and chat. There's a corner where a vending machine sells books, and news bulletins are projected onto a screen. Another night spot near the broadcasting studios on the Diagonal has a small TV screen on every table of its restaurant. Each design bar has its own theme so there should be something to suit the tastes of everyone.

Off the lower Ramblas and the Plaça Reial are clubs where flamenco singing and dancing are featured. Several large clubs with orchestras, dancing, floor shows, and restaurants are on the various "Barcelona by Night" tours that can be arranged through hotels. All these attractions can also be found in one place, the Poble Espanyol. In its

Barcelonans toot their horns at the fiestas.

alleys and plazas are jazz clubs, flamenco artists, big-band dancing, and discos going strong until 4:00 A.M.

FESTIVALS

Barcelonans work hard and play hard. Throughout the year, religious and secular holidays turn the different neighbourhoods or the whole city into a carnival. Food, fireworks, music, costumes, and especially the tall papier-mâché effigies called *gigantes* and their comical companions, the *cabezudo* walking heads, are essential fiesta features. Each neighbourhood has its own identifying models. The *gigantes* are about 4 metres (13 feet) high and are elaborately dressed as kings and queens, knights, ladies, gentlemen, and country folk. They are carried in stately procession by men and women concealed under costumes. The *cabezudos,* worn by youngsters or small adults, are usually oversize cartoon heads of well-known personalities or types. They prance about mischievously, accosting people in the crowd.

During many of these festivals, men and boys called *Castellers* climb on each other's shoulders to form human towers five or six men high in the Plaça de Sant Jaume. The topmost is a small boy who scampers like a monkey to reach up to the balcony of the Ajuntament city hall. Then the tower collapses gently from the top down.

With luck, one festival or another will be going on while you are in Barcelona. The box on page 94 lists the major events.

EATING OUT

All great chefs agree that ingredients make or break a cuisine. And anyone who has walked through one of Barcelona's great covered markets knows that the ingredients here are superb. As the city is a Mediterranean port, just-caught local fish and seafood take pride of place in Barcelona. Fruit and vegetables, known throughout Europe as imports from Spain, here are at their freshest. Mountain-cured hams and spicy sausages, spit-roasted meat and fowl with aromatic herbs, and umpteen kinds of omelettes are specialities. Barcelona's cosmopolitan population means you'll find restaurants featuring the food of every Spanish region (Basque cookery is especially appreciated) and from the rest of the world as well.

WHERE TO EAT

Barcelona restaurants run the full range from super-elegant to home-cooking. A grading system from five forks to one, marked on the door of the restaurant, is supposed to announce the category, though the signs are not always prominently displayed. The system is an indication of price and grades the elaborateness of the facilities and service, not the quality of the food. On weekday lunchtimes look out for the *menú del día* which usually offers the best bargain.

You can eat very well indeed never setting foot in a restaurant. The not-so-little snacks called *tapas* for which Barcelona bars and cafés are world famous come in dozens of delicious preparations, from appetizers such as olives and salted almonds to vegetable salads, fried squid, chilled shrimp, lobster mayonnaise, sausage slices, meatballs, spiced potatoes, cheese—almost anything the human frame requires to stave off hunger. The small plates are called a *porción*. A large serving is a *ración*, and half of this is a *media-ración*. You can easily get carried away into spending more on tapas than on a complete restaurant meal. But you can also eat tapas whenever you want, whereas restaurants serve lunch from about 1:00 to 3:30 P.M. and dinner from about 9:00 to 11:00 P.M.

WHAT TO EAT

Although it originates in rice-growing Valencia, the classic seafood *paella* (pronounced pie-ALE-ya) is probably high on every visitor's list of dishes to sample in Barcelona. Try the restaurants at La Barceloneta for a paella of fresh mussels, clams, shrimp, and several kinds of fish. It will take about 20 minutes to prepare.

A popular local fish served in many ways is *rape*, angler fish, tasty *a l'all cremat*, with burnt garlic. Other good bets are *mero al forn*, baked sea bass, and *llenguado a la graella* or *a la planxa*, a grilled sole. You might be fooled by *truita*, which means both trout and *tortilla*, the Spanish omelette. *Truita d'espàrrecs i alls tendres* is a delicious spring-time omelette of asparagus and young garlic. *Bacallà*, the lowly salt cod, is now served in the most distinguished restaurants in various transformations. Typically Catalan are *bacallà amb samfaina*, in a sauce resembling ratatouille, with onions, aubergine, tomato, courgettes, and peppers, and *esqueixada* (pronounced es-kay-SHA-da), which presents the cod shredded in a tart salad of beans, onions, olives, and tomato. A *sarsuela* is a stew of fish cooked in its own juices; a *graellada de peix* is a mixed grill of fish. Popular as a bar snack are *berberechos*, cockles. *Anxoves*, anchovies, find their way into many dishes.

Enjoy your meal!
Buen provecho —
(bwayn pro**vaych**oh)

A standard starter is the *pa amb tomàquet*, a solid slice of rough textured bread rubbed with the cut half of a fresh tomato and sprinkled with salt and a trickle of good olive oil. It can also be toasted or rubbed with onion or garlic. Other specialities to try are *llebre estofada amb xocolata*, stewed hare in a bittersweet chocolate sauce. There's a lobster version of this too. Barcelona's all-purpose sausage is the hearty *botifarra*, often served with *faves a la catalana*, broad beans stewed in an earthenware casse-

The ambiance of a Barcelona restaurant can be as exciting as the food.

role. The *xató* (pronounced sha-TO) endive and olives salad of Sitges is fortified with tuna (tunny) or cod, and has an especially good sauce made of red pepper, anchovies, garlic, and almonds ground to a paste with olive oil and vinegar. The word for salad of any kind is *amanida*. *Escalivada* is an aubergine, onion, and pepper salad. In *espinacs a la catalana*, spinach is mixed with *panses* (raisins) and pine nuts. Lots of mushrooms are found in the hills of Catalonia and the Pyrenees. Look for *moixernons* and the big, meaty *rovellons*.

When it comes to dessert, there'll always be the Spanish custard, *flan*, and the more liquid *crema catalana*. *Mel i mato* is a honey and creamy cheese treat. But the

Barcelona's Bars

The bar in Barcelona is much more than a saloon. It's an institution: restaurant, club, breakfast spot, place of entertainment, and ring-side seat on the passing parade. In its most recent manifestation, the "design bar" (see page 95), it serves as an architect's showcase. Every block in downtown Barcelona seems to have three or four bars. Some streets, along the Ramblas and in the port area, have one bar after another.

Typically, a bar has a counter with stools, plenty of standing room, and a wide open doorway so that passersby can see what's being offered inside. This will include an array of the hearty snacks called tapas, a row of dishes containing, at a minimum, anchovies, olives, shrimp, sardines, squid, potato salad, cured ham, salted almonds, and a cold omelette (*tortilla*) filled with sliced potatoes. Often bars will list their tapas on a blackboard on the sidewalk; a menu of 50 items is not unusual. The microwave oven has made even small bars capable of dishing up hot tapas.

The bar will serve coffee black (*solo*), with a spot of milk (*cortado*), or half hot milk (*con leche*), a glass of draught beer (*caña*), soft drinks, red and white wine by the glass, Spanish brandy (*copa*), and popular liqueurs, such as anis. Whiskies and gin drinks may be made with well-known brands produced under licence in Spain. Ask for a martini and you'll get a glass of vermouth. Some bars specialize in the local bubbly (*cava*), sold by the glass.

Barcelonans head for their local bars at mid-morning for a second breakfast, return for a luncheon spread of tapas, pop back again during the late afternoon and then after work to meet friends for a drink. When there's a football game on TV the bar will be crowded until the last whistle. Bars have their regulars, of course a *tertulia* is an informal group that gathers to discuss a special subject—art, football, or whatever.

greatest sweets are those delightful delicacies served in the ubiquitous pastry shops.

Drinks

Spanish wines are excellent. The best wines of the Rioja region in Navarre rank with very good Bordeaux, and justifiably cost as much, too. Every restaurant and bar has a house wine, usually from the Priorat or Penedés vineyards of Catalonia. This is what you'll get if you just say *tinto* (red) or *blanco* (white) as most diners do when asked for their choice of *vino*. You'll notice many of them pouring a bit of bubbly mineral water into the wine. This can smooth out a heavy or harsh wine.

Catalonia's sparkling *cava* is excellent and often sold to accompany a luscious dessert in pastry shops. Vintners learned how to make it from the French wineries they supplied with cork. Spanish dark beer on draft is first rate, too.

All sorts of spirits are widely available. Because many well-known brands are bottled under licence in Spain, they can be surprisingly cheap.

A popular non-alcoholic drink is *horchata de chufa*. This milky refresher has an almondy taste and is made from a sweet nut. *Horchaterías* are street bars that specialize in this cold drink and in ice-creams.

To Help You Order...

Could we have a table?	**¿Nos puede dar una mesa?**
Do you have a set menu?	**¿Tiene un menú del día?**
I'd like a/an/some…	**Quisiera…**

beer	**una cerveza**	milk	**leche**
bread	**pan**	mineral water	**agua mineral**
coffee	**un café**	napkin	**una servilleta**

cutlery	**los cubiertos**	potatoes	**patatas**
dessert	**un postre**	rice	**arroz**
fish	**pescado**	salad	**una ensalada**
fruit	**fruta**	sandwich	**un bocadillo**
glass	**un vaso**	sugar	**azúcar**
ice cream	**un helado**	tea	**un té**
meat	**carne**	(iced) water	**agua (fresca)**
menu	**la carta**	wine	**vino**

...and Read the Menu

aceitunas	**olives**	langosta	**spiny lobster**
albóndigas	**meat balls**	langostino	**large prawn**
almejas	**baby clams**	lomo	**loin**
atún	**tunny (tuna)**	mariscos	**shellfish**
bacalao	**codfish**	mejillones	**mussels**
besugo	**sea bream**	melocoton	**peach**
boquerones	**fresh anchovies**	merluza	**hake**
calamares	**squid**	ostras	**oysters**
callos	**tripe**	pastel	**cake**
cangrejo	**crab**	pimiento	**green pepper**
caracoles	**snails**	pollo	**chicken**
cerdo	**pork**	pulpitos	**baby octopus**
champiñones	**mushrooms**	queso	**cheese**
chorizo	**a spicy pork sausage**	salchichón	**salami**
		salmonete	**red mullet**
chuleta	**chops**	salsa	**sauce**
cocido	**stew**	ternera	**veal**
cordero	**lamb**	tortilla	**omelete**
entremeses	**hors-d'oeuvre**	trucha	**trout**
gambas	**prawns**	uvas	**grapes**
jamón	**ham**	verduras	**vegetables**
judías	**beans**		

INDEX

HANDY TRAVEL TIPS

An A–Z Summary of Practical Information

A

ACCOMMODATION *(hotel; alojamiento)*

The needs of the Olympic Games set off a much-needed hotel building boom in Barcelona. Even so, lodging in the best hotels is often hard to come by and advance reservations are strongly recommended. Spanish hostelries are graded by a star system, with five stars at the top. About two-thirds of the city's hotels fall in the four- and three-star categories. These classifications often seem arbitrary, with some two- and three-star places fully as good as others rated higher. Since hotel prices were freed from controls, charges have continued to rise and breakfast is rarely included in the room rate. Five- and four-star hotels are subject to 7 percent I.V.A. tax, lower categories, 6 percent.

For economy budgets, there are several hundred star-rated guest houses *(hostal, pensión)* and youth hostels *(albergue de juventud)*.

A list of all categories of accommodation may be obtained from the Spanish Tourist Offices in major capitals and cities and on arrival in Barcelona at tourist desks at the airport, railway station, and on the Moll de la Fusta quay at the foot of the Ramblas.

If possible, select a hotel not too far from the Plaça de Catalunya, a central point convenient for sightseeing and shopping on foot or by public transport.

I'd like	**Quisiera...**
a double/single room with/without bath/shower	**una habitación doble/sencilla con/sin baño/ducha**
What's the rate per night?	**¿Cuál es el precio por noche?**

AIRPORT *(aeropuerto)*

Barcelona's airport at El Prat de Llobregat is about 15 km (10 miles) from the city centre. Banks are open Monday to Friday 8:30 a.m to 2:30 p.m., Saturdays 8:30 a.m to 1 p.m. Tourist information and hotel reservation; Terminal A, Monday to Sunday 9:30 a.m. to 3:00 p.m., Terminal B, Monday to Saturday 9:30 a.m to 8 p.m., Sunday 9:30 a.m to 3 p.m.

Trains to Estació de Sants leave every 30 minutes, and buses to Plaça de Catalunya every 15 minutes. The train station is a bit far for passengers with heavy luggage, despite escalators and moving walkways, and arriving from the city you are unlikely to find the free baggage trolleys on the platform. Porters are available and there are plenty of taxis.

C

CAR HIRE *(coches de alquiler)*

The main international car-hire agencies have offices in Barcelona, and there are reputable Spanish agencies as well. Rates vary considerably so that it is worthwhile shopping around on arrival at the airport or, better still, before you go, when special package deals are often the cheapest. To rent a car, drivers must be over 21 years old and have a valid licence held for at least one year. Third-party insurance is automatically included, but taking out additional full collision coverage is advisable.

I'd like to rent a car (tomorrow)	**Quisiera alquilar un coche (para mañana).**
for one day/a week	**por un día/una semana**
Please include full insurance cover.	**Haga el favor de incluir el seguro a todo riesgo.**

CLIMATE and CLOTHING

Barcelona's mild Mediterranean climate assures sunshine most of the year and makes freezing temperatures rare even in the depths of winter, December through March. Spring and autumn are the most agreeable seasons. Mid-summer can be hot and humid. At times a thick smog hangs over the city.

From November through April you'll be wise to have a warm jacket or sweater and raincoat. The rest of the year, light summer clothing is in order. Men are expected to wear a jacket and tie in the better restaurants and nightclubs.

		J	F	M	A	M	J	J	A	S	O	N	D
average daily	°F	55	57	60	65	71	78	82	82	77	69	62	56
maximum*	°C	13	14	16	18	21	25	28	28	25	21	16	13
average daily	°F	43	45	48	52	57	65	69	69	66	58	51	46
minimum*	°C	6	7	9	11	14	18	21	21	19	15	11	8

* Minimum temperatures are measured just before sunrise, maximum temperatures in the afternoon.

COMMUNICATIONS

Main post offices provide facilities for sending telexes and telefaxes as well as a 24-hour telegram service. You usually can't make telephone calls from post offices (*correos*). The main Barcelona post office is in the port area at Plaça d'Antonio López. Hours are 8 a.m. to 9 p.m. weekdays and from 9 a.m. to 2 p.m. on Saturdays. Smaller branches are only open from 9 a.m. to 2 p.m. weekdays.

Mail. The general delivery or poste restante address in Barcelona is Lista de Correos, Plaça d'Antonio López, Barcelona 08003. The window is in the entry hall of the main post office. You'll need your passport or other identification and must pay a small charge for each letter received. Stamps are sold in tobacco shops and are usually available in hotels.

Telegrams (*telegrama*). The main telegram office is in the main post office in Plaça d'Antonio López, open daily from 8 a.m. to 9 p.m. Telegrams may be sent from the city's smaller post offices, or over the phone 24 hours a day by calling 322 20 00. International operators are linguists, but you can also ask your hotel to call in your telegram.

Telephone (*teléfono*). If you expect to make any international calls, find out how much extra your hotel charges above the regular rates listed in the front of the telephone directory. This may spare you an unpleasant surprise on your hotel bill. You can phone anywhere in the world from the phone booths on the street, and if you have looked up the rates in advance, you can calculate how much change you are going to need. Pick up the receiver and when you get the dial tone, dial 07; wait for a second dial tone to enter the country code, local code, and the number you are calling.

To reverse charges, you have to use an operator-manned kiosk (found at airports, seaside resorts, and at the Plaça de Catalunya central telephone exchange). To place a call to Europe and North America dial 005; within Spain 009.

Can you get me this number in...?   **¿Puede comunicarme con este número en...?**

Barcelona

Have you received any mail for...?	¿Ha recibido correo para...?
A stamp for this letter/postcard please.	Por favor, un sello para esta carta/tarjeta postal.
I would like to send a telegram to...	Quisiera mandar un telegrama a...

COMPLAINTS

Tourism is Spain's leading industry and the government takes complaints from tourists very seriously. The majority of disputes in hotels and restaurants are due to misunderstandings and linguistic difficulties and should not be exaggerated. As your host wants to keep both his reputation and his licence, you'll usually find him amenable to reason. In the event of a serious problem, you can demand a complaint form (Libro Oficial de Reclamaciones), which all hotels and restaurants are required by law to have available. The original of this triplicate document should be sent to the regional office of the Ministry of Tourism; one copy stays with the establishment against which the complaint is registered, and you keep the third.

Recent legislation greatly strengthens the consumer's hand. Public information offices are being set up, checks carried out, and fallacious information made punishable by law. For a tourist's need, however, the tourist office, or, in really serious cases, the police, would normally be able to handle it or, at least, to advise you where to go.

CONSULATES *(consulado)*

Almost all Western European countries have consulates in Barcelona. All embassies are located in Madrid.

Australia. Gran Vía Carles III 265, 10th floor; tel. 330 94 96
Canada. Passeig de Gràcia, 77 PO 3; tel. 215 07 04
Ireland. Gran Vía Carles de III, 94, 10th floor; tel. 491 50 21
U.K.* Avinguda Diagonal, 477; tel. 419 90 44
U.S.A. Paseo Elisenda de Montcada, 23; tel. 280 22 27
     * Also for citizens of Commonwealth countries

CRIME

The Barcelona Urban Security Council gives this advice: don't leave your luggage unattended; don't carry around more money than you'll need for daily expenses; use the hotel safe deposit for larger sums and valuables; in crowds around street attractions and sports events, be on your guard against pickpockets; reject offers of flowers or other objects from street pedlars—they may be after your purse; wear cameras strapped crosswise on the body; don't leave video cameras, radio cassettes, and valuables in view inside your car, even when locked; photocopy personal documents and leave the originals in your hotel. Once nominated the Olympic site, Barcelona began clearing the city centre streets of drug pushers, pickpockets, and other petty crooks preying on tourists. The blue-clad mobile regional anti-crime squads are out in force on the Ramblas and principal thoroughfares, with visible results. Should you be the victim of any theft or crime, report it at once to the nearest police station (comisaría) and to your consulate. Interpreters are posted at the Comisaria, Ramblas 43, tel. (93) 301 90 60. They are available daily from 7 a.m. to 11 p.m.

I want to report a theft.	**Quiero denunciar un robo.**
My handbag/ticket/wallet/	**Me han robado el bolso/**
passport has been stolen	**el billete/la cartera/el pasaporte.**

D

DRIVING

Crossing the border into Spain, you won't be asked for documents, but in the event of any problem you will have to produce a passport, a valid driver's licence, proper registration papers, and a "Green Card" extension of your regular car insurance to make it valid in foreign countries. This can be obtained from your insurance company. An International Driving Permit is useful if your licence does not include a translation in Spanish. Check with your automobile club for the latest information before your departure.

With your certificate of insurance, you are strongly recommended to carry a bail bond. If you injure someone in an accident in Spain, you can be imprisoned while the accident is being investigated. This bond will bail you out. Apply to your automobile association or insurance company.

Your car should display a nationality sticker. Seat belts are compulsory. Most fines for traffic offences are payable on the spot.

Barcelona

Parking. Don't take any chances parking "just for a minute" in a no parking area. You may come back to find a yellow triangular sticker affixed to the spot with instructions (in Catalan) on how to find your towed-away car. A heavy fine will await you.

In any event, there are many underground parking facilities and garages marked with a big blue-and-white "P" in the centre of the city, as well as clearly marked (in blue) sections of the side streets that parallel the main boulevards, with ticket vending machines (coin or credit-card operated) for up to two hours' parking (nights and Sundays excepted). Tickets have to be placed on the dashboard, visible from outside.

Speed limits. Maximum speed is 120 km/h (74 mph) on motorways, 100 km/h (62 mph) or 90 km/h (56 mph) on other roads, 60 km/h (37 mph) in towns and built-up areas. Cars towing caravans (trailers) are restricted to 80 km/h (50 mph) on the open road.

Fuel. Petrol (gasoline) stations are marked on city maps, and carry a full range of unleaded, super, normal, and diesel. A coin or two tip for the attendant is customary.

Fluid measures

Distance

Road signs. Most road signs are given in both Spanish and Catalan, accompanied by the standard symbols used throughout Europe.

(International) Driving Licence	**Carnet de conducir (internacional)**
Car-registration papers	**Permiso de circulación**
Green card	**Carta verde**
Are we on the right road for...?	**¿Es ésta la carretera hacia...?**

Full tank, please.	**Llene el depósito, por favor.**
normal/super/unleaded	**normal/super/sin plomo**
Please check the oil/tyres/battery.	**Por favor, controle el aceite/ los neumáticos/la batería.**
Can I park here?	**¿Puedo aparcar aquí?**
My car has broken down.	**Mi coche se ha estropeado.**
There's been an accident.	**Ha habido un accidente.**

E

ELECTRIC CURRENT *(corriente eléctrica)*

220 volts is standard, but some hotels have a voltage of 110–120 in bathrooms as a safety precaution. Check before plugging in any appliance.

Sockets (outlets) take round, two-pin plugs, so you will probably need an international adapter plug. Visitors from North America will need a transformer unless they have dual-voltage travel appliances.

What's the voltage?	**¿Que voltaje es?**
an adapter/a battery	**un transformador/una pila**

EMERGENCIES (See also CONSULATES, MEDICAL CARE, POLICE, and CRIME)

The National Police emergency number (in and outside Barcelona) is 091; dial 092 for the traffic police and 080 in the event of fire.

Careful!	**Cuidado**	Police!	**Policia**
Fire!	**Fuego**	Stop!	**Deténagase**
Help!	**Socorro**	Stop thief!	**Al ladrón**

ENTRY and CUSTOMS FORMALITIES *(aduana)*

Nationals of the U.S. and Canada need only a valid passport to visit Spain. The British may no longer enter on a visitor's passport—a full passport is needed. Visas are required for some Latin American and African countries, for Australia and New Zealand: check with your travel agent if in doubt. Persons coming from yellow fever or cholera zones may be required to produce an immunization card.

The chart below shows customs allowances for items of personal use. For E.U. residents there are no longer any restrictions on the movement of non–duty free goods for personal use between E.U.

countries. The amounts given under E.U. apply to the total amount of goods which can be taken into any E.U. country by non-E.U. residents, and the amount of goods which may be taken duty-free by E.U. residents into any other E.U. country.

Into:	Cigarettes		Cigars		Tobacco	Spirits		Wine
E.U.	200	or	50	or	250 g	1*l*	and	2*l*
Australia	200	or	250g	or	250 g	1*l*	or	1*l*
Canada	200	and	50	and	900 g	1.1*l*	or	1.1*l*
N. Zealand	200	or	50	or	250 g	1.1*l*	and	4.5*l*
S. Africa	400	and	50	and	250 g	1*l*	and	2*l*
U.S.A.	200	and	100	and	1)	1*l*	or	1*l*

1) A reasonable quantity. **Currency restrictions:** Visitors may bring up to one million pesetas into or out of the country without a declaration. If you intend to bring in and take out again larger sums, declare this on arrival and departure.

G

GUIDES (*guía*)

Licensed guides may be engaged through the Associació Professional d'Informadors Turístics de Barcelona; tel. 345 42 21. Hotels and travel agencies will also put you in touch with qualified guides and interpreters.

We'd like an English-speaking guide.	**Queremos un guía que hable inglés.**
I need an English interpreter.	**Necesito un intéprete de inglés.**

GETTING TO BARCELONA

If the choice of ways to go is bewildering, the complexity of fares and regulations can be downright stupefying. Consult a reliable travel agent for up-to-date information on the latest prices and timetables.

By Air. There are direct flights to Barcelona from most European capitals and major cities, as well as from various points in North America and North Africa. Flying times: London, about 2 hours; New York, approximately eight hours. Iberia, the Spanish national airline, covers most countries in shared arrangements with their own carriers. A regular air shuttle connects Barcelona and Madrid.

Consult your travel agent for the schedule of special flights, charters, and package deals on offer.

By Road. Drivers heading towards the Mediterranean on the French superhighway network cross into Spain south of Perpignan and join the Spanish autopista A-7 (toll motorway) at the frontier post of La Jonquera 150 km (93 miles) north of Barcelona. An alternative route from Toulouse over the Pyrenees enters Spain at Puigcerdà and follows the N-152 169 km (105 miles) to Barcelona. The narrow, twisting coastal road from the Port Bou border post provides lovely views of the Costa Brava. Regular coach services also operate from major European cities to Spain and are very comfortable and fast. During the summer many special services are offered with package deals.

By Rail. Passengers generally have to change trains at the Spanish frontier, as the Spanish tracks are of a wider gauge than the French. Exceptions are the luxury high-speed Talgo and the Trans-Europ-Express, which have adjustable axles. Significant discounts are applicable to Eurail Pass, Youth Pass, and Inter-Rail holders.

By Sea. For British travellers visiting Barcelona, a ferry links Plymouth and Santander in northern Spain (a 24-hour trip). From Santander, follow the N-240 to Barcelona.

L

LANGUAGE

Both Catalan and Castilian Spanish are official languages in Catalonia, and virtually all the people a traveller encounters will speak Spanish, even though regional government policy and the personal preference of native Barcelonans favour Catalan. Street signs are all in Catalan, museum labels and menus usually in both languages.

The European-minded Barcelonans frequently speak French, English, or Italian. Nevertheless, learning and using some courtesy phrases in Catalan will earn you a smile of appreciation. Here are a few:

ENGLISH	CATALAN	CASTILIAN
Good morning	**Bon dia**	*Buenos días*
Good afternoon	**Bona tarda**	*Buenos tardes*
Good night	**Bona nit**	*Buenos noches*

Barcelona

Thank you	**Gràcies**	*Gracias*
You're welcome	**De res**	*De nada*
Please	**Si us plau**	*Por favor*
Goodbye	**Adéu**	*Adiós*

The Berlitz SPANISH PHRASE BOOK AND DICTIONARY covers most situations you are likely to encounter during your stay in Barcelona. The Berlitz SPANISH-ENGLISH/ENGLISH-SPANISH pocket dictionary contains 12,500 concepts, plus a menu-reader supplement.

Do you speak English?	**¿Habla usted inglés?**
I don't speak Spanish.	**No hablo español.**

LAUNDRY *(lavandería)* **and DRY CLEANING** *(tintorería)*

Most hotels will do laundry the same day and dry-cleaning overnight, but they'll usually charge more than a laundry or a drycleaner.

Where's the nearest laundry/drycleaner?	**¿Dónde está la lavandería/tintorería más cercana?**
When will it be ready?	**¿Cuándo estará listo?**
I must have this for tomorrow morning.	**Lo necesito para mañana por la mañana.**

LOST PROPERTY

The office for *objetos perdidos* has the phone number 318 95 31. To report a lost credit card, phone American Express (91 572 03 03), Eurocard (91 519 21 00 or 91 519-60 00), Master Charge or Visa (315 25 12).

I've lost my wallet/handbag/ passport.	**He perdido mi cartera/bolso/ pasaporte.**

MAPS and STREET NAMES

Since 1985, all street names in Barcelona and most Catalan towns have been posted in Catalan. Towns have reverted to their Catalan names, too. Lérida is Lleida, San Carlos is Sant Carles, etc. Maps before this time may still have names in Spanish and even quite different names. Some words that may crop up frequently:

CATALAN	CASTILIAN	ENGLISH
Avinguda	**Avenida**	*Avenue*
Carrer	**Calle**	*Street*
Església	**Iglesia**	*Church*
Palau	**Palacio**	*Palace*
Passeig	**Paseo**	*Boulevard*
Passatge	**Pasaje**	*Passageway*
Plaça	**Plaza**	*Square*

Many Barcelona streets are one way and/or do not permit turns to the left or right. The give-away tourist maps do not have streets catalogued and keyed to the map. Buy a good street map and save time and trouble. The Guía Urbana de Barcelona handbook is most comprehensive and contains much useful information. The maps in this book were prepared by Falk-Verlag, Hamburg, who also publish a detailed map of Barcelona.

I'd like a street plan of...	**Quisiera un plano de la ciudad de...**
a road map of this region	**un mapa de carreteras de esta comarca**

MEDICAL CARE

There are several public first-aid stations (*Centros de Asistencia Primaria*) in different districts of Barcelona, mostly open roughly from 8 a.m. to 7 p.m. For medical emergencies turn to a first-aid station or call 061, which will arrange an ambulance or direct you to the nearest hospital. The better hotels have an arrangement with a doctor on call or can direct you to one of the private clinics.

A special Spanish health-and-accident insurance for tourists (ASTES) covering doctor's fees and clinical care is often available as part of a tourist package. Visitors from E.U. countries with corresponding health-insurance facilities are entitled to medical and hospital treatment under the Spanish social security system. Before leaving home, ensure that you are eligible and have the appropriate forms. It is recommended that you take out reputable private medical insurance, which will be part of almost all travel insurance packages.

Pharmacies (*farmacia*) operate during normal business hours but there is always one in every district that is open all night and on holidays. The location and phone number of this *farmacia de guardia* is posted on the door of all the other *farmacias*.

Contraception. With the growing problem of AIDS (SIDA), strong Roman Catholic opposition has been overcome and contraceptives are easily available from pharmacies, at public restrooms, and in other less likely places. The word for a condom is *preservativo*.

Where's the nearest (all-night) pharmacy?	**¿Donde está la farmacia (de guardia) más cercana?**
I need a doctor/dentist.	**Necesito un médico/dentista.**

MEETING PEOPLE

The people of Barcelona are genuinely friendly, proud of their city, and do not look contemptuously on people who speak their language badly. They'll go out of their way to give you directions. If you are male, it isn't difficult to start up conversations with your neighbour in a snack bar or bus by commenting on the fortunes of the Barça football team. Good manners dictate that when addressing anyone about anything at all, in person or on the telephone, you begin by saying "bon dia" or "buenos días," followed by senyor, senyora, or senyoreta, as appropriate. A handshake on greeting and leaving is normal.

MONEY MATTERS

Currency. The monetary unit of Spain is the peseta (abbreviated pta.).
- Banknotes: 1,000, 2,000, 5,000, 10,000 pesetas
- Coins: 1, 5, 10, 25, 50, 100, 200 and 500 pesetas

A 5-peseta coin is called a duro and prices are sometimes quoted in duros, e.g., 10 duros = 50 ptas.

Banking hours are traditionally from 8:30 a.m. to 2 p.m., Monday to Friday, Saturday 8:30 a.m. to 1 p.m. Throughout May to September banks remain closed on Saturdays. More and more banks now keep their central offices downtown open until 5 p.m. There is no rule on this, so take note of the times posted in the bank doors. Private money changers and travel agencies with a *cambio* sign will serve you outside banking hours.

There are money-changing facilities in the Sants and Término-França railway stations open daily all year from 8 a.m. to 10 p.m. On

Sundays, the Sants station office is closed between 2–4 p.m. The airport exchange counter is open every day from 7:15 a.m. to 10:45 p.m.

You will usually pay less commission on traveller's cheques than cash, and hotels and shops charge a considerable mark-up when changing money. Take your passport with you when changing money or cheques.

Credit cards. Internationally recognized cards are accepted by hotels, restaurants, and businesses in Spain, and you can even use some to pay tolls on the motorway. Check in advance whether yours is accepted.

Eurocheques. Most hotels and department stores take Eurocheques.

Where's the nearest bank/ currency exchange office?	**¿Donde está el banco/la oficina de cambio más cercana?**
I want to change some pounds/ dollars.	**Quiero cambiar libras/dólares.**
Do you accept travellers cheques?	**¿Aceptan cheques deviaje?**
Can I pay with this credit card?	**¿Puedo pagar con esta tarjeta de crédito?**

PLANNING YOUR BUDGET

To give you an idea of what to expect, here's a list of average prices in Spanish pesetas. However, they must be regarded as approximate and vulnerable to inflation.

Airport transfer. Train to city centre, 400 ptas. Bus, 450 Ptas.

Car hire. Economy car rates begin at 5,000 ptas. ($32) per day and 25,000 ptas. ($160) per week. These prices include unlimited mileage and third-party insurance. An extra charge is payable for comprehensive insurance, and 16% VAT is not included.

Entertainment. Cinema 650 ptas. and about 550 ptas. on Wednesdays at certain locations. Theatres 1,000–3,500 ptas., with special midweek rates. Flamenco nightclub 3,500–4,000 ptas. including one drink, 7,000–7,500 ptas. with dinner. Discotheque 1,500–2,000 ptas. with one drink. Poble Espanyol 950 ptas., children 7–14 years 450ptas.

Barcelona

Hairdressers. Woman's shampoo and set or blow-dry 2,500–3,500 ptas. Man's haircut 1,700–3,000 ptas.

Hotels. (double room with bath per night). *****23,000–50,000 ptas., **** 17,000–32,000 ptas., ***10,000–19,000 ptas., **9,500 ptas., *6,000 ptas. Add 6% or 7% I.V.A. (Value Added Tax).

Meals and drinks. Continental breakfast 500–1,700 ptas., three-course menu 900–2,000 ptas. including wine; lunch/dinner in a good restaurant 4,000–6,000 ptas.; beer 160 ptas., coffee 110–150 ptas., Spanish brandy 175–350 ptas., soft drink 160 ptas.

Metro or bus. 140 ptas.

Shopping bag. 500 g bread 150 ptas., 250 g of butter 200 ptas., dozen eggs 280 ptas., 1 kg. veal 1,800–2,500 ptas., 250 g of coffee 250 ptas., 1 litre of milk 150 ptas., bottle of wine from 225 ptas.

Taxi. Initial charge 300 ptas. for first 2 km. or six minutes, 100 ptas. per piece of luggage. A taxi from the airport to the city centre costs 2,000 ptas.

N

NEWSPAPERS and MAGAZINES *(periódico; revista)*

The many newsstands and bookstalls along the Ramblas carry the day's leading English, German, and French newspapers and The *International Herald Tribune*. A good selection of European and American magazines is also widely available in the city.

For Spanish-speakers or those willing to give it a try, the weekly entertainment information magazine *Guía del Ocio* (Leisure Guide) lists bars, restaurants, cinema, theatre, and concerts. For information about the city, try the magazines *Barcelona* and *Vivir en Barcelona* (Barcelona Life). All of the above are available at newsstands.

Have you any English-language newspapers/magazines? | **¿Tienen periódicos/revistas en inglés?**

O

OPENING HOURS

Barcelonans are not as addicted to the siesta as other Spaniards. The big department stores, some main bank branches, and shops remain open all day and factories also work full shifts. Other than this, very few shops open all day; usual hours are from 9:30 a.m. to 1:30. p.m. and 5 to 8 p.m. Monday to Saturday.

Government offices and the vast majority of businesses are open from 9 a.m. to 2 p.m. and from 3 p.m. to anywhere from 5:30 to 7 p.m. Restaurants start serving lunch around 1 p.m. until 3 p.m. and dinner from 8-9 p.m. until 11 p.m. or later.

P

PHOTOGRAPHY and VIDEO

Many shops in midtown will develop and print colour film in an hour or two. All popular brands of film are on sale. Customs regulations limit importing film to 10 rolls per camera.

Airport baggage scanners won't hurt your film, exposed or not.

A haze filter is a good investment and will protect your lens. Remember that noonday shots will have a bluish tone, while early morning and evening pictures overemphasize red.

I'd like a film for this camera. **Quisiera un carrete para esta máquina.**

How long will it take to develop (and print) this film? **¿Cuánto tardarán en revelar (y sacar copias de) este carrete?**

POLICE

There are three police forces: the Policía Municipal on traffic duty with white-and-blue-checked hat bands, the blue uniformed Policía Nacional, an anti-crime brigade that usually patrols in pairs or is motorized, and the Guardia Civil, a national force assigned to rural areas and recognizable by their patent leather hats (now being phased out). Interpreters are stationed at a few central police stations *(comisarías)*. See also CRIME.

Where's the nearest police station? **¿Dónde está la comisaría más cercana?**

Barcelona

PUBLIC HOLIDAYS *(Fiesta)*

Certain public holidays change from year to year. The local government publishes a list of holidays at the beginning of each year.

January 1	*Año Nuevo*	New Year's Day
January 6	*Día de Reyes*	Epiphany
May 1	*Día del Trabajo*	Labour Day
June 24	*San Juan*	St. John's Day
August 15	*Asunción*	Assumption
September 11	*Fiesta Nacional de Catalunya*	Catalonia National Day
September 24	*Día de la Mercè*	Day of our Lady of Mercy
November 1	*Todos los Santos*	All Saint's Day
December 6	*Día de la Constitución*	Constitution Day Española
December 8	*Inmaculada Concepción*	Immaculate Conception
December 25	*Navidad*	Christmas Day
December 26	*San Esteban*	St. Stephan's Day

Movable Dates:	*Viernes Santo*	Good Friday
	Lunes de Pascua	Easter Monday
	Lunes de Pentecostés	Pentecost

In addition there are special festivities in the different *barris* (districts) of Barcelona during the year, especially in late August.

R

RADIO and TELEVISION *(radio; televisión)*

National broadcasting on the two state-run channels is in Spanish, with one local station in Catalan. The better hotels have one or more satellite channels providing programmes in English, French, and German. Voice of America and the B.B.C. are received clearly on short wave.

RELIGIOUS SERVICES *(servicio religioso)*

Roman Catholic mass is said regularly in the churches of Barcelona, great and small. The French Parish at Carrer d'Anglí 15 occasionally has an English-language service (tel. 204 49 62). The Anglican church of St. George at Sant Joan de la Salle holds Sunday services at 11 a.m. The Greek Orthodox church is located at Carrer d'Aragó

181, the Jewish community synagogue is at Carrer de l'Avenir 24, and the Toarek Ben Ziad mosque is at Carrer Hospital 91.

T

TIME DIFFERENCES

Spanish time coincides with that of most of Western Europe—Greenwich Mean Time plus one hour. In spring, clocks are put forward an hour for Daylight Saving Time (Summer Time).

Summer Time Chart:

New York	London	**Spain**	Jo'burg	Sydney	Auckland
6 a.m.	11 a.m.	**noon**	noon	8 p.m.	10 p.m.

What time is it?   **¿Qué hora es?**

TIPPING

Service is almost always included in hotel and restaurant bills. If in doubt, ask "¿Está incluido el servicio?" A further tip of a few coins is appropriate. Follow the chart below for rough guidelines.

Airport or station porter	100 ptas. per bag
Hotel porter, per bag	200 ptas.
Maid, for extra services	100–200 ptas.
Waiter	5% (optional)
Taxi Driver	5%
Tourist guide	10%
Hairdresser	10%
Lavatory attendant	25–50 ptas.

TOILETS

There are many expressions for "toilets" in Spanish: *aseos, servicios, W.C.*, and *retretes*. The first two are the most common. Toilet doors are distinguished by a "C" for "*Caballeros*" (gentlemen) or "S" for "*Señoras*" (ladies) or by a variety of pictographs.

In addtion to the well-marked public toilets in the main squares and stations, a number of neat coin-operated toilets in portable cabins marked "W.C." are installed at convenient locations around the city. Just about every bar and restaurant has a toilet available for public use. It is considered polite to buy a drink if you drop in specifically to use the conveniences.

Where are the toilets? **¿Dónde están los servicios?**

TOURIST INFORMATION OFFICES *(oficinas de turismo)*

Spain maintains tourist offices in many countries. These offices will supply you with a wide range of colourful and informative brochures and maps in English. If you visit one, you can consult a copy of the master directory of hotels in Spain, listing all facilities and prices.

Australia
• International House, Suite 44, 104 Bathurst St., P.O. Box A-675, 2000 Sydney NSW; tel. (02) 264 79 66

Canada
• 102 Bloor St. West, 14th floor, Toronto, Ont., M5W 1M8; tel. (416) 961 31 31

United Kingdom
• 57-58 St. James's St., London SW1A 1LD; tel. (0171) 499 1169

United States
• Water Tower Place, Suite 915 East, 845 North Michigan Ave., Chicago IL, 60611; tel. (312) 642-1992
• 1221 Brickell Avenue, Miami, FL 33131; tel. (305) 358 1992
• 8383 Wilshire Blvd., Suite 960, Beverly Hills, CA 90211; tel. (213) 658-7188/93
• 666 Fifth Ave., New York, NY 10103; tel. (212) 265-8822

Barcelona
At the Barcelona airport, at railway stations and on the Moll de la Fusta on the quay at the foot of the Ramblas, information and hotel reservation desks with multi-lingual staff can help you get oriented and provide a programme of events for the month. The city's main office of tourism is at Plaça de Catalunya and is open from 9 a.m. to 9 p.m. daily.

The Ajuntament (City Hall) citizen's information phone number around the clock is 010. There are also electronic bulletin boards at strategic locations that list sporting and cultural events and other information continuously.

Where is the tourist office? **¿Dónde está la oficina de turismo?**

TRANSPORT

Barcelona has an excellent network of buses, metro lines, funiculars, a suburban railway, and a lovely old blue tram, a relic that goes part way up Mount Tibidabo. In the Plaça de Catalunya, a point where many lines start or converge, you can buy combination ten-ride tickets good on all facilities (except for train stops outside the city, such as the airport) and at the same time pick up a free map of these services. Using this ticket on the automatic machines at the front of the buses and at metro turnstiles saves time. The same ticket can be used for your whole family—just have it punched once for each person up to ten times. During the summer, one-, three-, and five-day tickets for unlimited rides are also available. You can, of course, buy (more expensive) single tickets from the bus driver or from metro, funicular, or tram ticket booths. Ten-ride tickets can only be bought in the Plaça de Catalunya, at metro stations, in "Caixes" (savings banks), or at a few major banks.

A very good bet from June 24 to September 15 is the "Barcelona Singular" combination ticket covering all services and the bus Number 100. This bus leaves the Pla del Palau every 45 minutes and follows a special touristic route all over the city. In 90 minutes it covers most of the places you'll want to visit, and you can hop on and off as often as you wish.

Metro. Barcelona's underground railway crosses the city more rapidly than other forms of transport and runs from 5 a.m. to 11 p.m. weekdays and to 1 a.m. on Friday and Saturday and the day before public holidays. On holidays service is from 6 a.m. to 11 p.m., on Sundays from 6 a.m. to midnight. The station entrances are marked with a red diamond outlining the word "metro."

Buses. Bus stops are covered and list the numbers and routes of the buses on that route, including the hours of service. Most buses run from 5:30 a.m. to 11:30 p.m., but on the main routes some run all night long. If you're waiting for a bus after 10 p.m., better check the timetable.

Taxis are black with yellow trim and there are lots on the streets at all hours. A green light and/or a *libre* (vacant) sign shows when the cab is empty. Taxis bear the initials "*S.P.*" (servicio público) on front and rear.

Ferries connect Barcelona to Palma de Mallorca daily and serve Menorca and Ibiza six times a week in summer. A weekend cruise operated from March until June by the Compañia Transmediterránea runs to Palma, stopping at Ibiza, using the ship as a hotel for 2 nights (tel. 443 2532).

Trains. Spain's national railway, the RENFE *(Red Nacional de Ferrocarriles Españoles)* operates fast and punctual long-distance trains throughout the peninsula and to international connecting points. Seat reservations are essential during holidays and the summer season. Tickets may be bought in travel agencies as well as in the central Sants station. Most trains stop for passengers in midtown at the Passeig de Gràcia underground station, useful for travellers with a hotel in the Eixample district. The Estació de França in the harbour area is the station used for local trains going up the coast and, since recent expansion works, for many international trains.

The Generalitat de Catalunya (regional government) operates local trains to the suburbs, including points of interest to tourists. These run on the same tracks as metro lines. The train to Montserrat and Manresa leaves from the Plaça d'Espanya. The Plaça de Catalunya station serves the Autonomous University of Barcelona, Sant Cugat, and Terrassa.

RENFE honours Inter-Rail, Rail-Europ, and Eurail cards (the latter sold only outside Europe), and offers other discounts to youths (under 26) and seniors (over 65). Many discounts reach 50 percent. Anyone intending to use the train to reach Barcelona or to travel outside it will do well to find out about current discount tickets from a travel agency, local railway station, or, in Barcelona, from the information desk in the central station or by phoning RENFE (322 41 42).

When's the next bus/train to...?	**¿Cuándo sale el próximo autobús/ tren para...?**
A ticket to...	**Un billete para...**
single (one way)	**ida**
return (round trip)	**ida y vuelta**
What's the fare to...?	**¿Cuánto es la tarifa a...?**
first/second class	**primera/segunda clase**

W

WATER

Barcelona's water is safe, but it is so heavily chlorinated as to be almost unpalatable. Good bottled water is available, fizzy (*con gas*) or flat (*sin gas*), and some shops even sell this water in plastic bubbles to make unchlorinated ice cubes.

a bottle of mineral water	**una botella de agua mineral**
Is this drinking water?	**¿El agua es potable?**

WEIGHTS and MEASURES

Spain uses the metric system.

Length

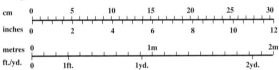

Weight

Temperature

NUMBERS

0	cero	11	once	30	treinta
1	uno	12	doce	40	cuarenta
2	dos	13	trece	50	cincuenta
3	tres	14	catorce	60	sesenta
4	cuatro	15	quince	70	setenta

Country

5	cinco	16	dieciséis	80	ochenta
6	seis	17	diecisiete	90	noventa
7	siete	18	dieciocho	100	cien
8	ocho	19	diecinueve	101	ciento uno
9	nueve	20	veinte	500	quinientos
10	diez	21	veintiuno	1,000	mil

DAYS OF THE WEEK

Sunday	**domingo**	Thursday	**jueves**
Monday	**lunes**	Friday	**viernes**
Tuesday	**martes**	Saturday	**sábado**
Wednesday	**miércoles**		

SOME USEFUL EXPRESSIONS

yes/no	**sí/no**
please/thank you	**por favor/gracias**
excuse me/you're welcome	**perdone/de nada**
where/when/how	**dónde/cuándo/cómo**
yesterday/today/tomorrow	**ayer/hoy/mañana**
day/week/month/year	**día/semana/mes/año**
left/right/up/down	**izquierda/derecha/arriba/abajo**
good/bad	**bueno/malo**
big/small	**grande/pequeño**
hot/cold	**caliente/frío**
old/new	**viejo/nuevo**
open/closed	**abierto/cerrado**
early/late	**temprano/tarde**

Does anyone here speak English?	**¿Hay alguien aquí que hable inglés?**
What does this mean?	**¿Qué quiere decir esto?**
I don't understand.	**No comprendo.**
Please write it down.	**Escríbamelo, por favor.**
Is there an admission charge?	**¿Se debe pagar la entrada?**
I'd like...	**Quisiera...**
How much is that?	**¿Cuánto es?**
Help me, please.	**Ayúdeme, por favor.**
Get a doctor quickly!	**¡Llamen a un médico, rápidamente!**

Recommended Hotels

In the following pages, we offer a sampling of recommended establishments in Barcelona. The list is by no means exhaustive, but is designed to provide a few pointers to help you when making your choice.

Hotels have been selected according to their facilities and location, and whether they offer something extra in the way of charm, picturesque setting, or historic associations. The number of stars for each hotel is awarded under the Spanish grading system (see page 107). We have divided the hotels into the following price ranges, based on the cost of a double room with bath or shower.

Higher-priced above ptas.   20,000 | | |
Medium-priced ptas.   10,000-20,000 | |
Lower-priced up to ptas.   10,000 |

We cannot guarantee the accuracy of these prices, which should be used as an approximate guide only.

Alexandra ✪✪✪✪ *Mallorca 251, 08008 Barcelona; Tel. 487 0505; fax 488 0258.* 75 rooms. | | |

Aragón ✪✪✪ *Aragó 569 bis, 08026 Barcelona; Tel. 245 89 05; fax 247 09 23.* 78 rooms. | |

Arenas ✪✪✪✪ *Capità Arenas 20, 08034 Barcelona; Tel. 280 0303, 280 53 72; fax 280 3392.* 59 rooms. | |

Arts ✪✪✪✪✪ *Marina 19, 08005 Barcelona; Tel. 221 10 00; fax 221 10 70.* 455 rooms. Luxury hotel by the sea in the Olympic Village, with spectacular views of the city. | | |

Avenida Palace ✪✪✪✪ *Gran Vía de les Corts Catalanes 605–607, 08007 Barcelona; Tel. 301 96 00; fax 318 12 34.* 159 rooms. Deluxe hotel. Excellent, attractive service. | | |

Barcelona

Barcelona ✪✪✪✪ *Casp 1, 08010 Barcelona; Tel. 302 58 58; fax 301 86 74.* 72 rooms. Central location. ❚ ❚

Bonanova Park ✪✪ *Capità Arenas 51, 08034 Barcelona; Tel. 204 09 00; fax 204 50 14.* 60 rooms. ❚

Colón ✪✪✪✪ *Avda. Catedral 7, 08002 Barcelona; Tel. 301 14 04; fax 317 29 15.* 147 rooms. ❚ ❚

Condes de Barcelona ✪✪✪✪ *Passeig de Gràcia 75, 08008 Barcelona; Tel. 488 22 003; fax 487 14 42.* 183 rooms. Modern, centrally located hotel in beautiful setting. Impeccable facilities and service. ❚ ❚ ❚

Cortés ✪✪ *Santa Ana 25, 08002 Barcelona; Tel. 317 92 12, 301 33 96; fax 302 78 70.* 46 rooms. Central location. ❚

Covadonga ✪✪✪ *Avda. Diagonal 596, 08021 Barcelona; Tel. 209 55 11; fax 209 58 33.* 85 rooms. ❚

Cristal ✪✪✪✪ *Diputació 257, 08007 Barcelona; Tel. 487 87 78; fax 487 90 30.* 148 rooms. ❚ ❚

Derby ✪✪✪✪ *Loreto 21, 08029 Barcelona; Tel. 322 32 15.* 40 rooms. Exceptionally pleasant. ❚ ❚ ❚

Diplomatic ✪✪✪✪ *Pau Claris 122, 08009 Barcelona; Tel. 488 02 00; fax 488 12 22.* 215 rooms. Swimming pool. ❚ ❚ ❚

España ✪✪ *Sant Pau 9–11, 08001 Barcelona; Tel. 318 17 58; fax 317 11 34.* 73 rooms. ❚

Gaudí ✪✪✪ *Nou de la Rambla 12, 08001 Barcelona; Tel. 317 90 32; fax 412 26 36.* 71 rooms. Central location. ❚

Ginebra ✪ *Rambla de Catalunya 1, 08007 Barcelona; Tel. 317 10 63; fax 317 55 65.* 10 rooms. ❚

Gótico ✪✪✪ *Jaume I, 14, 08002 Barcelona; Tel. 315 22 11; fax 310 40 81.* 81 rooms. Picturesque, central location. ❚ ❚

Gran Vía ✪✪✪ *Gran Vía de les Corts Catalanes 642, 08007 Barcelona; Tel. 318 19 00; fax 318 99 97.* 48 rooms. Historic building. ▮

Gran Hotel Calderón ✪✪✪✪ *Rambla de Catalunya 26, 08007 Barcelona; Tel. 301 00 00; fax 412 41 93.* 244 rooms. Indoor and outdoor swimming pools. ▮ ▮ ▮

Hilton ✪✪✪✪✪ *Avda. Diagonal 589-591, 08014 Barcelona; Tel. 495 77 77; fax 495 57 00.* 290 rooms. Modern hotel. ▮ ▮ ▮

Le Meridien Barcelona ✪✪✪✪ *Rambla 111, 08002 Barcelona; Tel. 318 62 00; fax 301 77 76.* 208 rooms. Central location. ▮ ▮ ▮

Lléo ✪✪✪ *Pelai 24, 08001 Barcelona; Tel. 318 13 12; fax 412 26 57.* 42 rooms. Central location. ▮

Majéstic ✪✪✪✪ *Passeig de Gràcia 70, 08008 Barcelona; Tel. 488 17 17; fax 488 18 80.* 350 rooms. Picturesque, central location. Swimming pool, terrace. ▮ ▮ ▮

Melià Barcelona Sarrià ✪✪✪✪ *Avda. de Sarrià 50, 08029 Barcelona; Tel. 410 60 60; fax 321 51 79.* 314 rooms. Modern hotel. ▮ ▮ ▮

Numància ✪✪✪ *Numància 72–74, 08029 Barcelona; Tel. 322 44 51; fax 410 76 42.* 140 rooms. ▮ ▮

Park Hotel ✪✪✪ *Avda. Marquès de l'Argentera 11, 08003 Barcelona; Tel. 319 60 00; fax 319 45 19.* 87 rooms. ▮

Princess Sofia ✪✪✪✪✪ *Plaça Pius XII 4, 08028 Barcelona; Tel. 330 71 11; fax 330 76 21.* 505 rooms. Luxury hotel. Picturesque setting, terrace. Swimming pool. ▮ ▮ ▮

Rallye ✪✪✪ *Travessera de les Corts 150, 08028 Barcelona; Tel. 339 90 50; fax 411 07 90.* 104 rooms. Swimming pool. ▮ ▮

Barcelona

Regencia Colón ✪✪✪ *Sagristans 13–17, 08002 Barcelona;
Tel. 318 98 58; fax 317 28 22.* 55 rooms. Historic building. ▮ ▮

Regente ✪✪✪✪ *Rambla de Catalunya 76, 08008 Barcelona;
Tel. 487 59 89; fax 487 32 27.* 78 rooms. Modernist style,
rooftop swimming pool. ▮ ▮

Ritz ✪✪✪✪✪ *Gran Vía de les Corts Catalanes 668, 08010
Barcelona; Tel. 318 52 00; fax 318 01 48.* 197 rooms. Central
location. ▮ ▮ ▮

Royal ✪✪✪✪ *La Rambla 117, 08002 Barcelona; Tel. 301 94
00; fax 317 31 79.* 108 rooms. Central location with picturesque
setting. ▮ ▮

San Agustín ✪✪✪ *Plaça de Sant Agustí 3, 08001 Barcelona;
Tel. 318 1658; fax 317 29 28.* 76 rooms. Picturesque, central
location. ▮

Suizo ✪✪✪ *Plaça de l'Angel 12, 08002 Barcelona; Tel. 315
04 60; fax 310 40 81.* 50 rooms. Comfortable, modest hotel in
central location. ▮ ▮

Tryp Presidente ✪✪✪✪ *Avda. Diagonal 570, 08021
Barcelona; Tel. 200 21 11; fax 209 51 06.* 161 rooms. Modern
hotel with a range of luxury facilities. Swimming pool. ▮ ▮ ▮

Toledano ✪ *Rambla 138 PO4, 08002 Barcelona; Tel. 301
0872; fax 412 31 42.* 17 rooms. Central location. ▮

Via Augusta ✪✪ *Via Augusta 63, 08006 Barcelona; Tel. 217
92 50; fax 237 7714.* 44 rooms. ▮

Recommended Restaurants

Our criteria for restaurants are quality of cuisine, ambiance, and service. For each address we mention any special features, and regular closing days, if any. Most restaurants also have periods of annual closing, usually in August, at Christmas, and at Easter. Phoning ahead to check is always wise, as is advance reservation. We have grouped the restaurants also into three categories according to price. Prices reflect the cost of an à la carte three-course meal without drinks.

Higher-priced above ptas.	5,000	✪✪✪
Medium-priced ptas.	3,000-5,000	✪✪
Lower-priced up to ptas.	3,000	✪

A la Menta ✪✪✪ *Passeig Manuel Girona 50, 08034 Barcelona; Tel. 204 15 49.* Seafood. Closed Sunday evenings.

Agut ✪ *Gignàs 0016, 08002 Barcelona; Tel. 315 17 09.* Traditional Catalan cuisine, popular with locals.

Aitor ✪✪ *Carbonell 5 (Barceloneta), 08003 Barcelona; Tel. 319 94 88.* Basque cuisine. Closed on Sundays.

Amaya ✪✪ *Rambla de Santa Mónica 0020–0024, 08002 Barcelona; Tel. 302 10 37.* Catalan-Basque cuisine.

Antigua Casa Solé ✪ *Sant Carles 4 (Barceloneta), 08003 Barcelona; Tel. 221 50 12.* Seafood specialities. Closed on Saturday evenings and all day on Sundays.

Asador de Aranda ✪✪ *Avda. Tibidabo 31, Barcelona; Tel. 417 01 15.* Castilian cuisine in Art Nouveau decor. Closed on Sunday evenings.

Bel Air ✪✪✪ *Córcega 286, 08008 Barcelona; Tel. 237 75 88.* Rice specialities. Closed on Sundays.

Barcelona

Botafumeiro ✪✪✪ *Gran de Grácia 81, 08012 Barcelona; Tel. 218 42 30.* Notably good cuisine, particularly the seafood specialities. Closed on Mondays and during August.

Brasserie Flo ✪✪✪ *Jonqueres 0010, 08003 Barcelona; Tel. 319 31 02.* French and Catalan cuisine. Excellent quality.

Ca l'Isidre ✪✪✪ *Les Flors 0012, 08001 Barcelona; Tel. 441 11 39.* Catalan cuisine in the bohemian atmosphere of the Paralelo, with Catalan art on the walls. Closed on Sundays.

Can Culleretes ✪ *Quintana 0050, 08002 Barcelona; Tel. 317 30 22.* Oldest restaurant in Barcelona. Excellent value. Closed on Sunday evenings.

Can Jaume ✪ *Avda. Pau Casals 10, 08021 Barcelona; Tel. 200 63 58.* Home-style cooking offering particularly good value. Closed on Saturday evenings and on Sundays.

Can Majó ✪✪ *Almirall Aixada 0023 (Barceloneta), 08003 Barcelona; Tel. 221 54 55.* Rice and seafood specialities. Good cuisine. Closed on Sunday evenings.

Can Punyetes ✪ *Maria Cugì 0189; Tel. 200 91 59.* Restaurant specializing in Catalan cuisine, open every day.

El Gran Café ✪✪ *Avinyó 9, 08002 Barcelona; Tel. 318 79 86.* French and Catalan cuisine. Piano music. Closed on Sundays.

Eldorado Petit ✪✪✪ *Dolors Monserdá 51; Tel. 204 51 53.* Traditional Catalan dishes and nueva cocina.

Finisterre ✪✪✪ *Avda. Diagonal 469, 08036 Barcelona; Tel. 430 91 14.* Excellent cuisine and service.

Gargantua i Pantagruel ✪✪ *Aragón 214, 08011 Barcelona; Tel. 453 20 20.* Good value. Closed on Sundays.

Gorría ✪✪ *Diputació 421, 08013 Barcelona; Tel. 245 11 64.* Excellent Basque-Navarre cuisine. Reservations essential. Closed on Sundays.

Jaume de Provença ✪✪✪ *Provença 88, 08029 Barcelona; Tel. 430 00 29.* Notably good nueva cocina and excellent service. Closed on Sunday evenings and on Mondays.

L'Olivé ✪ *Muntaner 171, 08036 Barcelona; Tel. 430 90 27.* Catalan cuisine. Reservations essential. Closed on Sunday evenings.

Los Caracoles ✪✪✪ *Escudellers 14, 08002 Barcelona; Tel. 301 20 41.* Regional country-style decor.

Marcos ✪ *Bonavista 10, 08012 Barcelona; Tel. 237 60 99.* Good cuisine. Friendly atmosphere. Closed on Saturday evenings and on Sundays.

Moncho's de Barcelona ✪✪ *Travessera de Gràcia 44–46, 08021 Barcelona; Tel. 414 66 22.* Seafood self-service buffet and grill.

Neichel ✪✪✪ *Avda. de Pedralbes 16 bis, 08034 Barcelona; Tel. 203 84 08.* Excellent cuisine and elegant restaurant–one of the best in Spain. Desserts are particularly good. Closed on Sundays.

Orotava ✪✪✪ *Consell de Cent 335, 08007 Barcelona; Tel. 302 31 28.* Game specialities. Notably good cuisine. Closed on Sundays.

Petit Punyalada ✪✪ *Poble Espanyol, Plaçeta de l'Esglesia 1; Tel. 423 03 15.* Catalan and French cuisine. Excellent view. Closed on Sunday evenings and all day on Mondays.

Reno ✪✪✪ *Tuset 27, 08006 Barcelona; Tel. 200 13 90, 200 91 29.* Excellent cuisine. Very elegant. Closed at Saturday midday.

Sa Lletuga ✪ *Mozart 4, 08012 Barcelona; Tel. 237 96 31.* Good cuisine. Closed on Sundays and Mondays.

Set Puertas ✪✪ *Passeig d'Isabel II, 14, 08003 Barcelona; Tel. 319 30 33.* Crowded, noisy, informal. Near the waterfront.

Via Veneto ✪✪✪ *Ganduxer 10–12, 08021 Barcelona; Tel. 200 72 44.* Considered one of the best restaurants in Barcelona. Belle Epoque decor. Closed at Saturday midday and on Sundays.

ABOUT BERLITZ

In 1878 Professor Maximilian Berlitz had a revolutionary idea about making language learning accessible and enjoyable. One hundred and twenty years later these same principles are still successfully at work.

For language instruction, translation and inter-pretation services, cross-cultural training, study abroad programs, and an array of publishing products and additional services, visit any one of our more than 350 Berlitz Centers in over 40 countries.

Please consult your local telephone directory for the Berlitz Center nearest you or visit our web site at http://www.berlitz.com.

Helping the World Communicate